MathFlare

Name: ______________________

Class: __________

Teacher: ______________________

Copyright © 2024 MathFlare Publishing.
All rights reserved. This book or any portion thereof may not be reproduced or used in any manner whatsoever without the express written permission of the publisher except for the use of brief quotations in a book review.

Introduction

As parents and educators, we recognize the pivotal role mathematics plays in shaping a child's academic journey and future success. Yet, the path to mathematical proficiency can often seem daunting, fraught with challenges and complexities. That's where the transformative power of MathFlare Workbooks shine through, illuminating the way forward with clarity, precision, and purpose.

Introducing MathFlare Workbooks – a beacon of guidance, a testament to excellence, and a catalyst for achievement. Crafted with meticulous care and expertise, MathFlare Workbooks stand as paragons of educational excellence, designed to nurture young minds, ignite a passion for learning, and develop a deep-rooted understanding of mathematical concepts.

Picture this: your child eagerly delves into the pages of Mathflare Workbook, greeted by a step-by-step guide illuminated with vivid examples that demystify complex mathematical concepts. With each turn of the page, they embark on a journey of discovery, encountering thoughtfully curated practice questions that reinforce learning and hone problem-solving skills. And when they unveil the answers to those very questions, a sense of accomplishment blossoms within them – a tangible reward for their hard work and dedication.

But MathFlare Workbooks are more than just tools for learning; they are pathways to comprehension, fostering a deep-seated understanding of mathematical concepts through a sequential, logical flow. From fundamental principles to advanced problem-solving strategies, every chapter builds upon the last, ensuring a robust foundation upon which future knowledge can be constructed.

As parents, we yearn for nothing more than to see our children thrive, to witness the spark of inspiration ignited within them as they conquer academic challenges with confidence and poise. MathFlare Workbooks serve as partners in this noble endeavor, offering not just practice questions, but the keys to unlocking a world of opportunity.

And for teachers, MathFlare Workbooks stand as invaluable allies in the quest to cultivate mathematical proficiency in the classroom. With answers readily available, instructors can focus on guiding and nurturing their students, confident in the knowledge that MathFlare Workbooks provide a solid framework upon which to build.

In the pages of MathFlare Workbooks, we find not just the promise of academic excellence, but the seeds of a brighter tomorrow. So let us embrace the power of mathematics, let us champion the journey of learning, and let us pave the way for a generation of young minds poised to shape the world. With MathFlare Workbooks as our guide, the possibilities are infinite, and the future, bright.

Table of Contents

MathFlare
Grade 2
MATH WORKBOOK
Addition
Subtraction
Multiplication
Place Value and Expanded Notations
Geometry
MathFlare Publishing

MathFlare
Grade 2-3
MATH WORKBOOK
Step by Step Guide and Essential Practice with Answers
Addition
Subtraction
Multiplication and Division
Place Value and Expanded Notations
Geometry
MathFlare Publishing

MathFlare
Grade 3
MATH WORKBOOK
Step by Step Guide and Essential Practice with Answers
Multiplication and Division
Decimals
Place Value and Expanded Notations
Fractions and Geometry
MathFlare Publishing

MathFlare
Grade 1
MATH WORKBOOK
Step by Step Guide and Essential Practice with Answers
Counting and Numbers
Addition and Subtraction
Place Value and Expanded Notations
Understanding Time
MathFlare Publishing

MathFlare
Grade 1-2
MATH WORKBOOK
Step by Step Guide and Essential Practice with Answers
Counting and Numbers
Addition and Subtraction
Place Value and Expanded Notations
Understanding Time
MathFlare Publishing

MathFlare
Grade 3-4
MATH WORKBOOK
Step by Step Guide and Essential Practice with Answers
Addition
Subtraction
Multiplication
Division
Place Value and Expanded Notations
Fractions and Geometry
MathFlare Publishing

MathFlare
Grade 4
MATH WORKBOOK
Step by Step Guide and Essential Practice with Answers
Addition
Subtraction
Multiplication
Division
Place Value and Expanded Notations
Fractions and Geometry
MathFlare Publishing

MathFlare
Grade 4-5
MATH WORKBOOK
Step by Step Guide and Essential Practice with Answers
Multiplication
Division
Place Value and Expanded Notations
Fractions and Geometry
Unit Conversion
MathFlare Publishing

MathFlare
MATH WORKBOOK
Grade 5
Step by Step Guide and Essential Practice with Answers
Multiplication Division
Place Value and Expanded Notations
Fractions and Geometry
Unit Conversion
MathFlare Publishing

MathFlare
MATH WORKBOOK
Grade 5-6
Step by Step Guide and Essential Practice with Answers
Multiplication Division
Place Value and Expanded Notations
Fractions and Geometry
Units and Statistics
MathFlare Publishing

MathFlare
MATH WORKBOOK
Grade 6
Step by Step Guide and Essential Practice with Answers
Integers and Statistics
Arithmetic and Pre-Algebra
Fractions and Geometry
Ratio and Percentage
MathFlare Publishing

MathFlare
MATH WORKBOOK
Grade 6-7
Step by Step Guide and Essential Practice with Answers
Arithmetic and Pre-Algebra
Ratio, Percent Proportion
Geometry
Statistics
MathFlare Publishing

MathFlare
MATH WORKBOOK
Grade 7
Step by Step Guide and Essential Practice with Answers
Pre-Algebra
Ratio, Percent Proportion
Geometry
Statistics
MathFlare Publishing

MathFlare
MATH WORKBOOK
Grade 7-8
Step by Step Guide and Essential Practice with Answers
Pre-Algebra
Ratio, Percent Proportion
Geometry and Cartesian Plane
Statistics
MathFlare Publishing

MathFlare
MATH WORKBOOK
Grade 8-9
Step by Step Guide and Essential Practice with Answers
Pre-Algebra
Ratio, Proportion and Percentage
Linear Equations
Geometry and Cartesian Plane
MathFlare Publishing

MathFlare
MATH WORKBOOK
Grade 8
Step by Step Guide and Essential Practice with Answers
Pre-Algebra
Percentage
Linear Equations
Geometry
MathFlare Publishing

Decimals

Adding Decimals

Adding decimals is like adding whole numbers, but we must align the decimal points carefully. For instance, when adding 49.88 and 45.78:

Step 1: Align the decimal points.

$$49.88$$
$$+\ 45.78$$

Step 2: Start adding from the rightmost digit (the ones place) and move to the left.

Add 8 and 8: 8 + 8 = 16. Write down 6 in the ones place and carry over 1 to the tenths place.

$$49.88$$
$$+\ 45.78$$
$$6$$

Step 3: Add the tenths place.

Add 1 (carried over from the previous step), 8, and 7: 1 + 8 + 7 = 16. Write down 6 in the tenths place and carry over 1 to the hundredths place.

$$49.88$$
$$+\ 45.78$$
$$66$$

$$49.88$$
$$+\ 45.78$$
$$9566$$

<u>Step 5: Finally, write the sum with the decimal point directly below the decimal points in the original numbers.</u>

$$49.88$$
$$+\ 45.78$$
$$95.66$$

Subtracting Decimals

Subtracting decimals follows a process like adding decimals, except instead of adding the numbers, we subtract them.

Let's solve more problems:

$$176.07$$
$$+\ 765.69$$
$$941.76$$

$$738.71$$
$$-\ 715.74$$
$$22.97$$

Multiplying Decimals

Multiplying decimals is a lot like multiplying whole numbers, but we need to be careful about where we put the decimal point in the answer.

Step 1: Start by multiplying the numbers together, just like we do with whole numbers. Ignore the decimals for now.

Step 2: Count how many decimal places there are in the numbers we're multiplying. This will tell us how many decimal places our answer should have.

Step 3: Put the decimal point in the answer by starting from the right side of the number. Move the decimal point to the left as many places as there are in the total number of decimal places.

For example, let's multiply 4.5 by 2.5:

Step 1: Multiply the numbers as if they were whole numbers:

$$25 \times 45 = 1125.$$

Step 2: There is one decimal place in 2.5 and one in 4.5, making a total of two decimal places.
Step 3: Starting from the right side of the answer, count two places to the left and put the decimal point there.

So, the final answer is 11.25.

Remember to pay close attention to where the decimal point goes in the answer.

Let's solve a problem:

$$22.93 \times 4.69$$

```
        2 2 . 9 3
    ×      4 . 6 9
    ________________
    +  2 0 6 3 7
    + 1 3 7 5 8
    +   9 1 7 2
    ________________
    = 1 0 7 5 4 1 7
```

Rewrite the product with
4 decimal places.
So the answer is **107.5417**

Dividing Decimals

Dividing decimals is a lot like dividing whole numbers, but we need to be careful about placement of decimal point in the answer.

Steps to follow:

1. **Set up the division problem:** Write the dividend (the number being divided) and the divisor (the number you're dividing by) as you would in a long division problem.

$$1.7 \overline{)1.6}$$

2. **Move the decimal:** Move the decimal point to the right in the dividend and divisor by the same number of places.

$$17\overline{)16}$$

3. **Perform the division:** Divide as you would with whole numbers.

$$
\begin{array}{r}
0\,0.9\,4 \\
17\overline{)16} \\
-\,0 \\
\hline
16 \\
-\,0 \\
\hline
16\,0 \\
-15\,3 \\
\hline
7\,0 \\
-6\,8 \\
\hline
2
\end{array}
$$

4. **Place the decimal point:** Place the decimal point in the quotient directly above its position in the dividend.

So, the quotient is 0.94.

Fractions

Fractions represent parts of a whole. They consist of a numerator (the number on top) and a denominator (the number on the bottom).

For example: we have an orange, and we divide it into 5 equal slices. Each slice represents $\frac{1}{5}$ of the orange. Now, if we take 3 of those slices, we have taken $\frac{3}{5}$ of the orange.

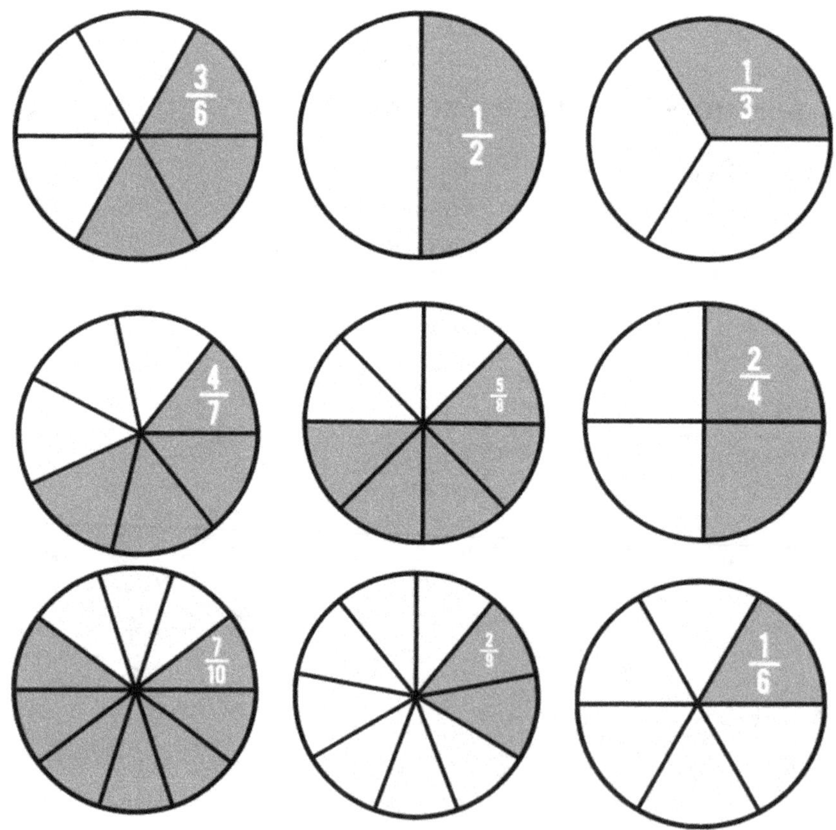

<u>Equivalent Fractions</u>

Equivalent fractions are fractions that represent the same value or part of a whole, even though they may look different.

To find equivalent fractions, you can:

- Multiply or divide both the numerator and denominator by the same nonzero number.
- Simplify fractions to their simplest form.

$\frac{1}{2}$ and $\frac{2}{4}$ are equivalent fractions because if you multiply the numerator and denominator of $\frac{1}{2}$ by 2, you get $\frac{2}{4}$. Similarly, if you divide both the numerator and denominator of $\frac{2}{4}$ by 2, you get $\frac{1}{2}$.

Let's solve a problem:

$$\frac{\ }{8} = \frac{15}{40}$$

To solve the missing numerator, we can cross multiply.

$$40x = 8 \times 15$$

$$40x = 120$$

$$x = \frac{120}{40} = x = 3$$

$$\frac{3}{8} = \frac{15}{40}$$

Fractions Addition (Common Denominator)

To add fractions with a common denominator, we add their numerators together and keep the denominator the same.

For example: if we want to add $\frac{3}{5}$ and $\frac{2}{5}$ both fractions have the same denominator of 5.

Therefore, to add them, we simply add their numerators:

$$\frac{3}{5} + \frac{2}{5} = \frac{3+2}{5} = \frac{5}{5}$$

Let's solve a problem:

$$\frac{9}{17} + \frac{1}{17} = \frac{9+1}{17} = \frac{10}{17}$$

Fractions Subtraction (Common Denominator)

To subtract fractions with a common denominator, we find the difference between their numerators and keep the denominator the same.

For example:

$$\frac{3}{5} - \frac{2}{5} = \frac{3-2}{5} = \frac{1}{5}$$

Let's solve a problem:

$$\frac{15}{16} - \frac{12}{16} = \frac{15-12}{16} = \frac{3}{16}$$

Fractions Multiplication

To multiply fractions, we simply multiply the numerators together to get the new numerator and multiply the denominators together to get the new denominator.

For example, let's multiply: $\dfrac{2}{4} \times \dfrac{1}{4}$

Numerator: 2 × 1 = 2

Denominator: 4 × 4 = 16

Therefore, $\dfrac{2}{16}$

we can simplify the resulting fraction:

$$\dfrac{1}{8}$$

Let's solve a problem:

$$\dfrac{4}{5} \times \dfrac{4}{5} = \dfrac{4 \times 4}{5 \times 5} = \dfrac{16}{25}$$

Fractions Division

To divide fractions, we multiply by the reciprocal of the divisor.

For example, let's divide:

$$\dfrac{6}{8} \div \dfrac{4}{8}$$

$$\dfrac{6}{8} \times \dfrac{8}{4} = \dfrac{48}{32} = \dfrac{3}{2}$$

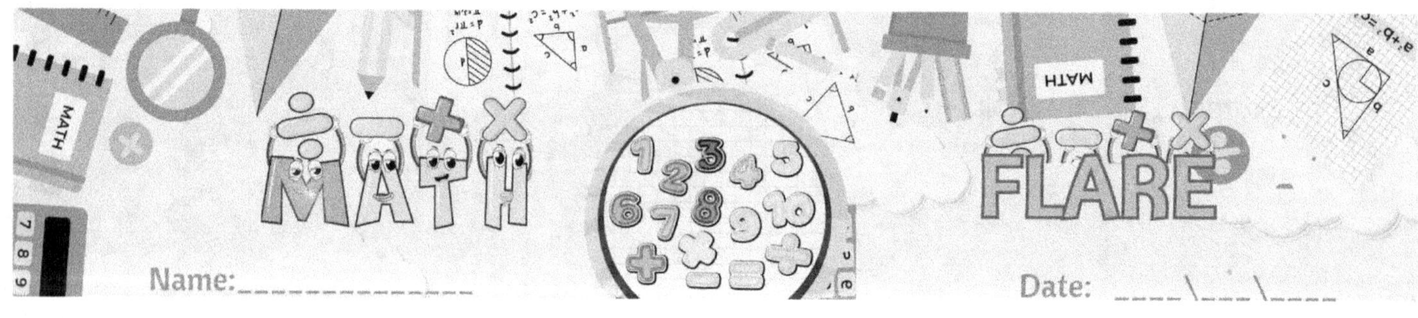

Adding Decimals

Find the sum.

1. 486.46
    + 954.05

2. 698.47
    + 334.29

3. 694.57
    + 826.09

4. 503.18
    + 390.37

5. 493.73
    + 149.03

6. 349.53
    + 553.49

7. 736.64
    + 998.99

8. 682.14
    + 710.72

9. 574.90
    + 120.56

10. 460.25
    + 332.04

11. 658.66
    + 827.56

12. 608.39
    + 494.23

13. 625.30
    + 322.22

14. 775.63
    + 328.01

15. 699.76
    + 507.89

16. 635.40
    + 963.32

17. 812.20
    + 210.19

18. 625.61
    + 245.39

19. 581.52
    + 694.40

20. 306.45
    + 387.03

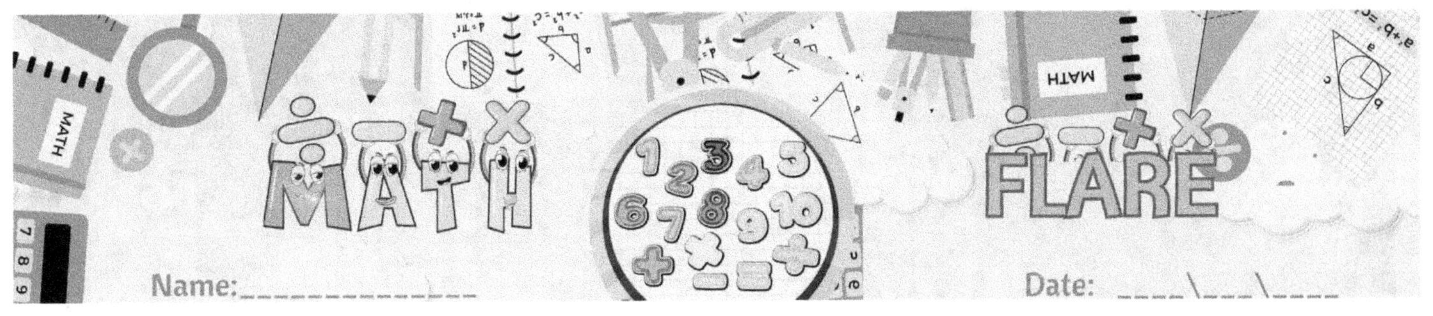

21.   226.21
 + 314.30
____

22.   274.40
 + 704.59
____

23.   429.73
 + 466.28
____

24.   880.45
 + 938.79
____

25.   383.92
 + 641.12
____

26.   653.15
 + 861.80
____

27.   470.69
 + 139.12
____

28.   904.84
 + 658.90
____

29.   445.67
 + 304.24
____

30.   708.97
 + 472.35
____

31.   150.46
 + 275.17
____

32.   690.59
 + 985.83
____

33.   513.62
 + 386.20
____

34.   741.28
 + 626.45
____

35.   473.38
 + 536.76
____

36.   229.20
 + 880.50
____

37.   814.10
 + 173.21
____

38.   205.83
 + 444.35
____

39.   653.15
 + 903.79
____

40.   164.50
 + 259.02
____

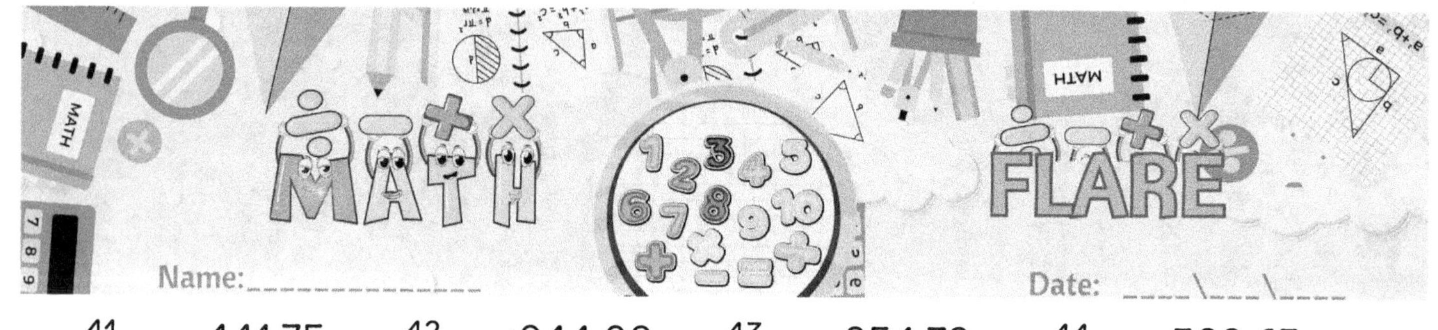

Name: __________________ Date: ____ \ ____ \ ____

41. 441.75 + 836.83	42. 944.09 + 158.64	43. 854.72 + 773.59	44. 592.63 + 773.07
45. 305.34 + 966.70	46. 799.71 + 377.28	47. 985.41 + 834.09	48. 336.57 + 951.04
49. 623.70 + 288.56	50. 290.97 + 143.53	51. 724.99 + 354.00	52. 565.41 + 847.15
53. 511.93 + 772.65	54. 147.70 + 397.48	55. 933.28 + 560.48	56. 105.74 + 541.87
57. 239.74 + 549.95	58. 130.60 + 313.62	59. 331.07 + 631.95	60. 231.11 + 740.01

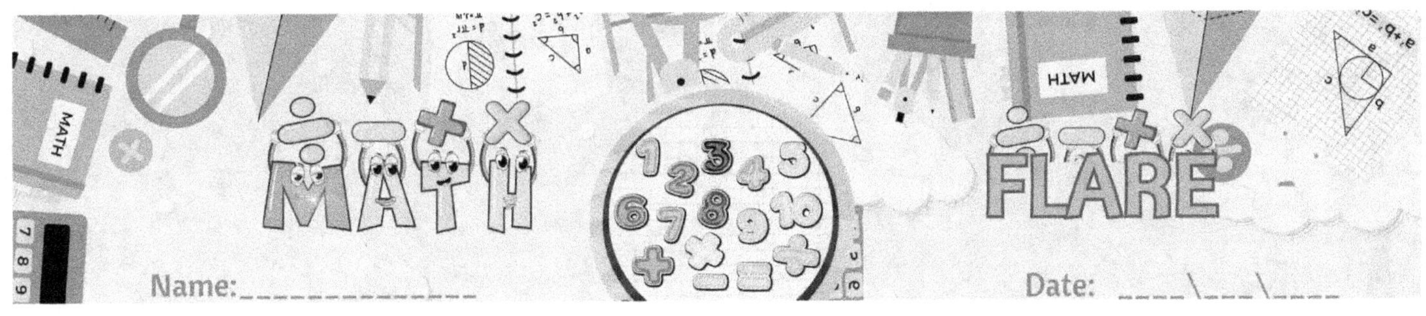

Subtracting Decimals

Find the difference.

61. 447.77 − 338.65	62. 787.97 − 729.43	63. 844.51 − 455.86	64. 864.09 − 167.12
65. 671.25 − 225.87	66. 950.42 − 695.53	67. 940.05 − 415.83	68. 822.40 − 398.67
69. 725.03 − 119.45	70. 699.66 − 355.89	71. 817.59 − 194.07	72. 670.99 − 280.85
73. 438.52 − 107.92	74. 263.91 − 180.92	75. 887.44 − 561.19	76. 685.36 − 487.10
77. 780.47 − 350.03	78. 577.89 − 575.26	79. 942.14 − 428.29	80. 957.52 − 157.97

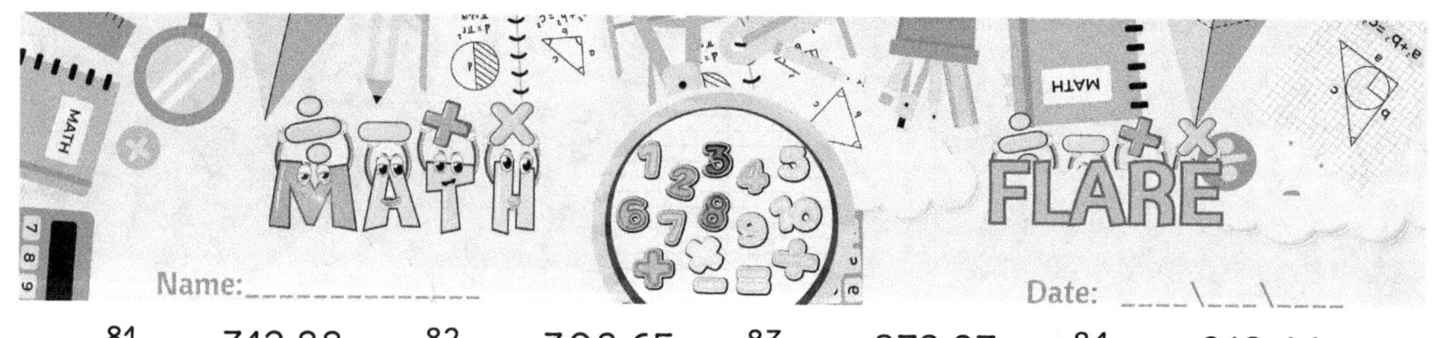

81. 312.88 − 312.50	82. 308.65 − 291.71	83. 972.87 − 522.85	84. 919.44 − 342.65
85. 492.06 − 110.49	86. 311.71 − 208.18	87. 784.23 − 374.01	88. 800.50 − 398.01
89. 415.94 − 266.54	90. 849.31 − 497.09	91. 904.07 − 826.55	92. 668.12 − 160.25
93. 960.18 − 163.33	94. 764.09 − 128.86	95. 252.04 − 221.49	96. 475.91 − 204.68
97. 565.51 − 489.91	98. 959.60 − 340.23	99. 738.65 − 731.45	100. 606.09 − 604.09

101. 636.56 − 557.46	102. 772.43 − 720.83	103. 246.01 − 174.81	104. 951.83 − 532.09
105. 701.03 − 459.33	106. 554.16 − 456.00	107. 932.15 − 880.18	108. 772.24 − 257.09
109. 568.11 − 407.92	110. 461.54 − 121.98	111. 567.81 − 117.76	112. 662.63 − 133.93
113. 557.40 − 542.53	114. 807.97 − 271.32	115. 717.70 − 416.36	116. 788.73 − 729.61
117. 999.38 − 988.80	118. 159.72 − 135.41	119. 196.01 − 170.20	120. 803.73 − 333.09

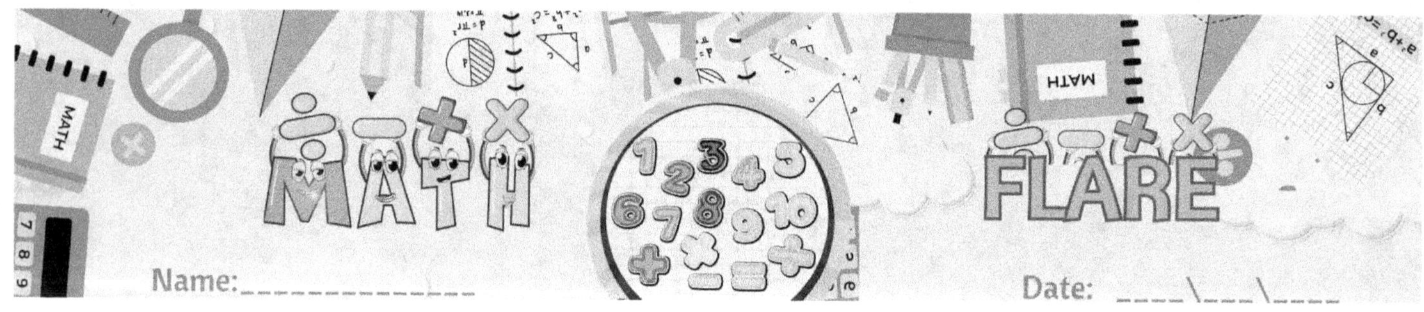

Multiplying Decimals

Find the product.

121.
40.5
× 16.8

122.
86.6
× 72.7

123.
68.8
× 52.7

124.
60.3
× 69.2

125.
14.1
× 65.9

126.
95.4
× 47.2

127.
76.3
× 72.3

128.
98.0
× 84.2

129.
25.8
× 96.9

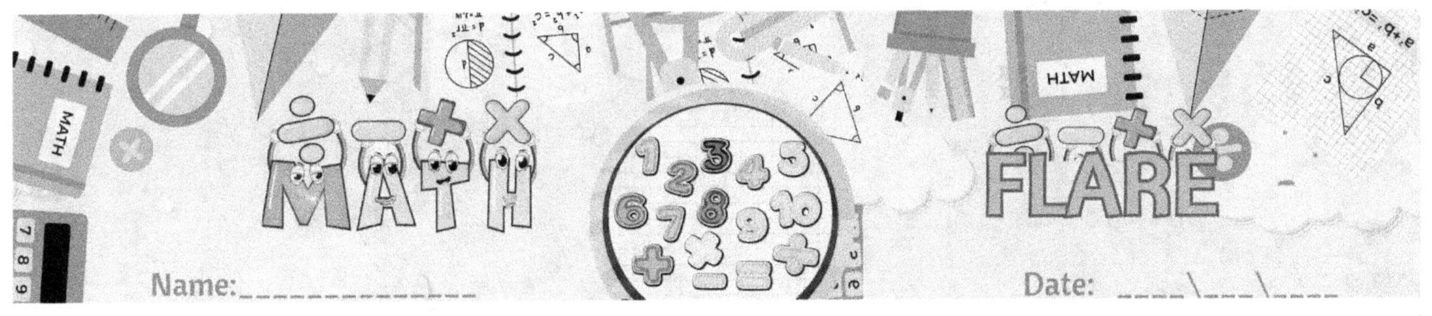

130. 97.7
× 24.8

131. 16.5
× 82.1

132. 92.2
× 52.1

133. 52.7
× 69.9

134. 96.2
× 31.0

135. 25.9
× 63.3

136. 44.7
× 94.3

137. 88.6
× 42.0

138. 19.6
× 41.8

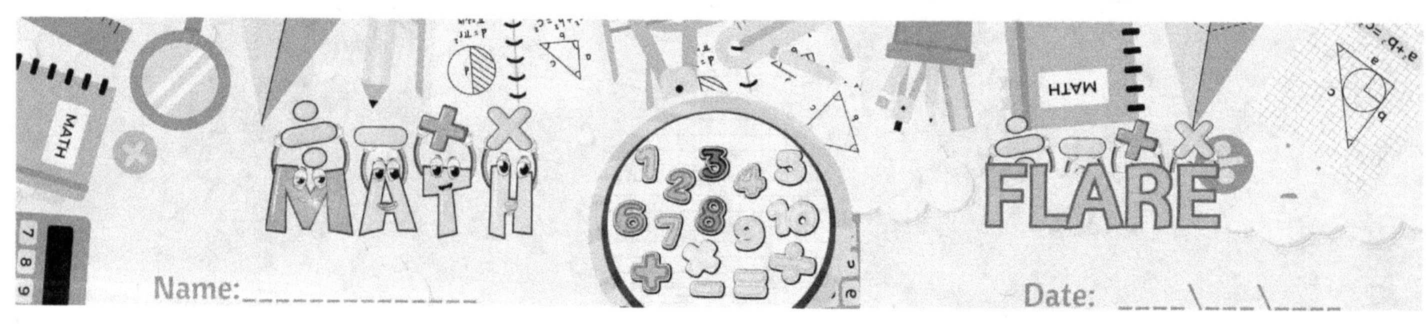

139. 98.3
    × 34.7

140. 32.6
    × 76.3

141. 56.1
    × 21.4

142. 77.6
    × 29.1

143. 98.2
    × 65.4

144. 73.2
    × 73.7

145. 99.3
    × 79.5

146. 96.1
    × 72.7

147. 31.6
    × 69.0

148. 74.1
    × 58.4

149. 24.5
    × 44.5

150. 29.9
    × 98.8

151. 56.4
    × 39.3

152. 53.3
    × 50.6

153. 31.2
    × 11.1

154. 58.5
    × 44.3

155. 62.7
    × 66.3

156. 85.7
    × 91.1

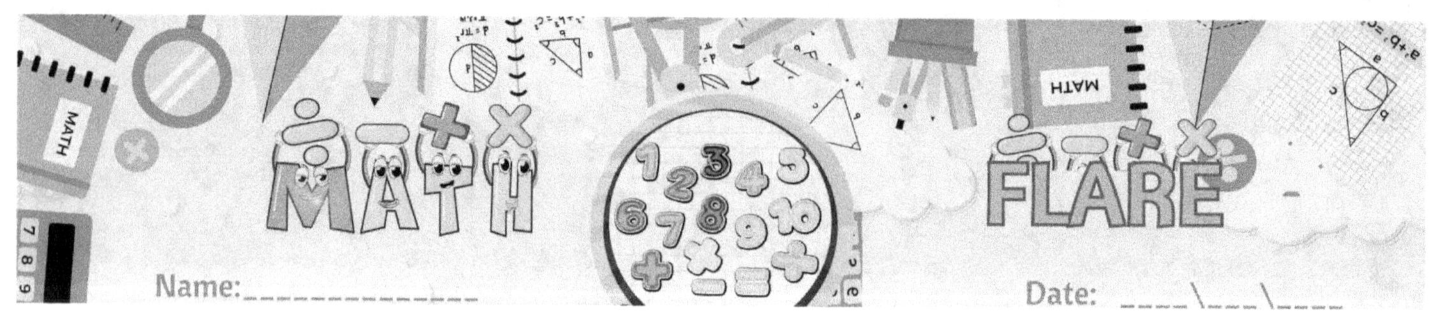

157. 74.3
    × 31.4

158. 68.6
    × 95.0

159. 14.5
    × 73.0

160. 53.7
    × 87.3

161. 96.6
    × 32.6

162. 31.7
    × 46.2

163. 67.1
    × 71.9

164. 72.6
    × 29.6

165. 67.8
    × 61.1

166. 27.2
    × 63.8

167. 14.7
    × 33.8

168. 30.0
    × 26.8

169. 68.0
    × 36.9

170. 97.8
    × 97.1

171. 16.8
    × 38.9

172. 20.9
    × 43.0

173. 93.7
    × 15.0

174. 98.3
    × 10.2

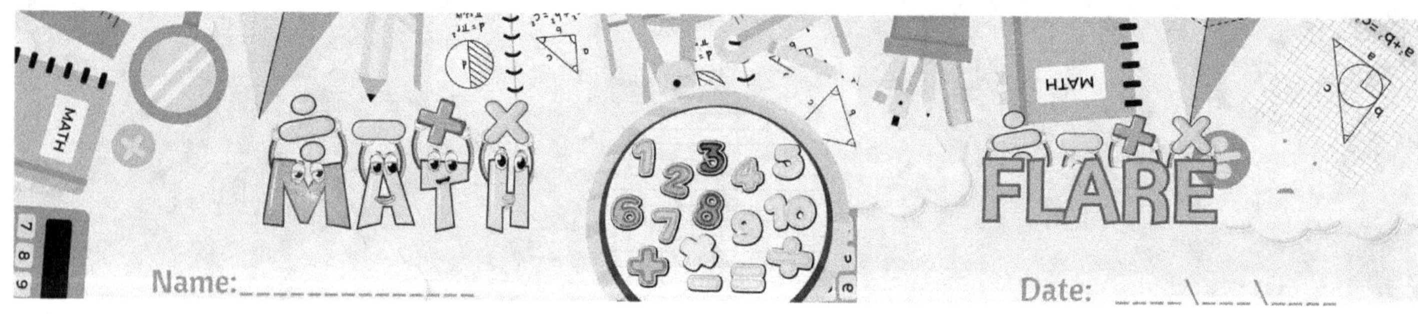

Dividing Decimals
Find the quotient.

175.

$$5 \overline{)75.1}$$

176.

$$2 \overline{)83.4}$$

177.

$$6 \overline{)45.8}$$

178.

$$2 \overline{)51.6}$$

179.

$$9 \overline{)95.4}$$

180.

$$10 \overline{)19.6}$$

181.

$$5 \overline{)34.2}$$

182.

$$4 \overline{)86.2}$$

183.

$$6 \overline{)55.2}$$

184.

$$2\overline{)24.0}$$

185.

$$4\overline{)87.1}$$

186.

$$10\overline{)82.7}$$

187.

$$10\overline{)97.1}$$

188.

$$10\overline{)92.4}$$

189.

$$5\overline{)43.6}$$

190.

$$9\overline{)29.0}$$

191.

$$2\overline{)14.0}$$

192.

$$4\overline{)14.6}$$

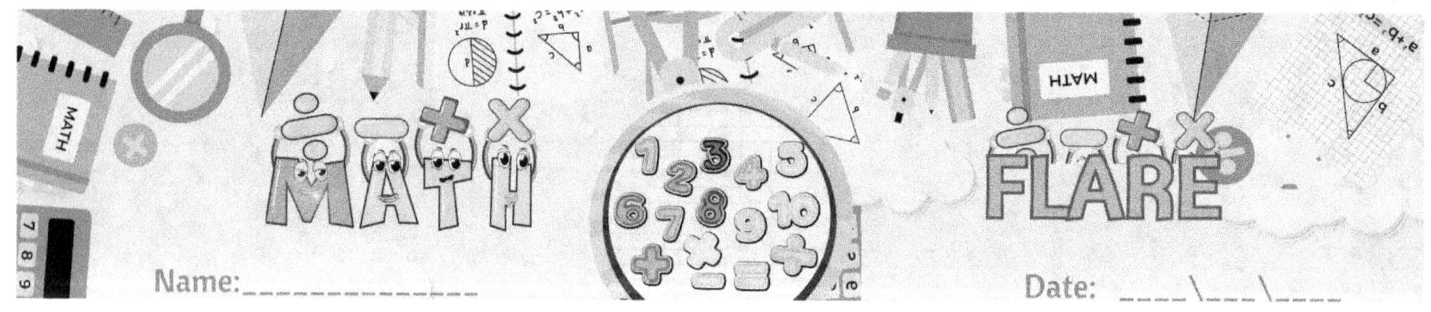

193.

$$4\overline{)40.3}$$

194.

$$3\overline{)17.7}$$

195.

$$8\overline{)15.6}$$

196.

$$8\overline{)72.3}$$

197.

$$8\overline{)70.8}$$

198.

$$6\overline{)91.4}$$

199.

$$8\overline{)49.7}$$

200.

$$8\overline{)29.3}$$

201.

$$9\overline{)75.2}$$

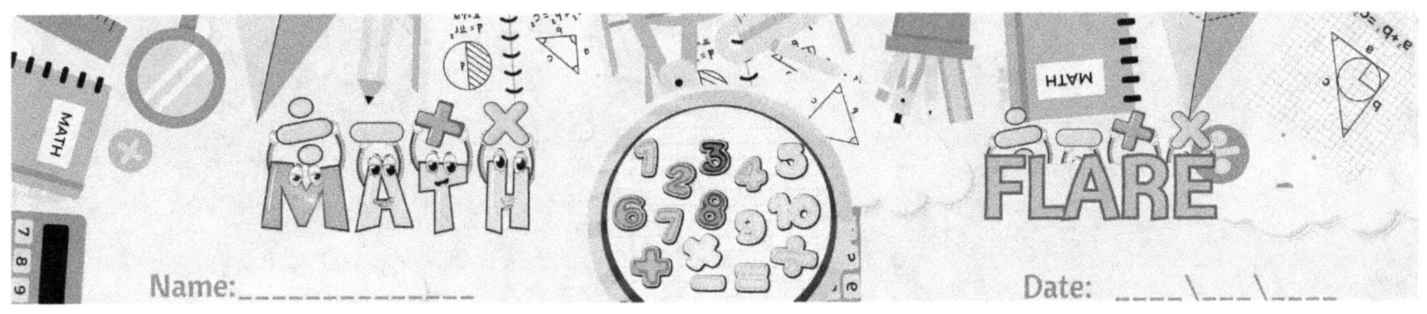

202.

$5 \overline{)93.8}$

203.

$9 \overline{)65.3}$

204.

$5 \overline{)23.6}$

205.

$6 \overline{)66.8}$

206.

$5 \overline{)71.8}$

207.

$3 \overline{)66.9}$

208.

$2 \overline{)94.5}$

209.

$6 \overline{)49.8}$

210.

$3 \overline{)12.9}$

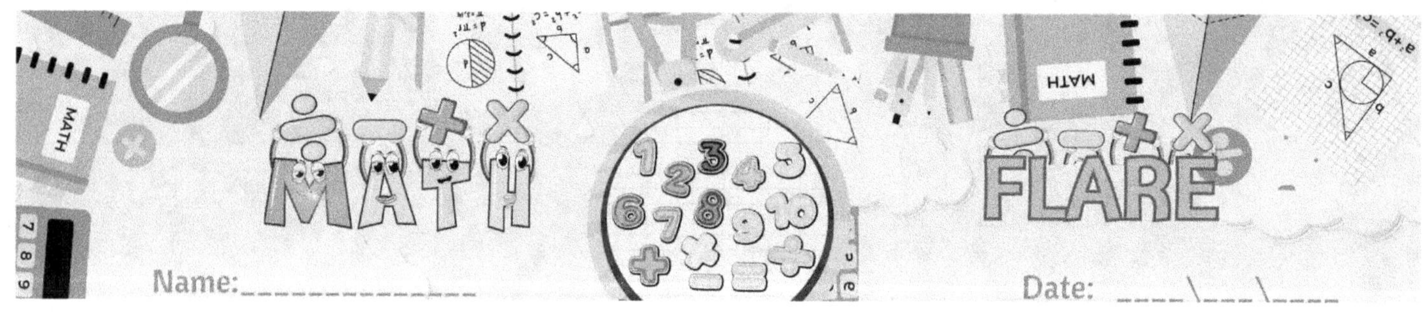

211.

$$9 \overline{)48.6}$$

212.

$$2 \overline{)19.4}$$

213.

$$1 \overline{)65.5}$$

214.

$$3 \overline{)35.0}$$

215.

$$4 \overline{)17.6}$$

216.

$$6 \overline{)56.7}$$

217.

$$5 \overline{)32.6}$$

218.

$$2 \overline{)28.9}$$

219.

$$7 \overline{)29.7}$$

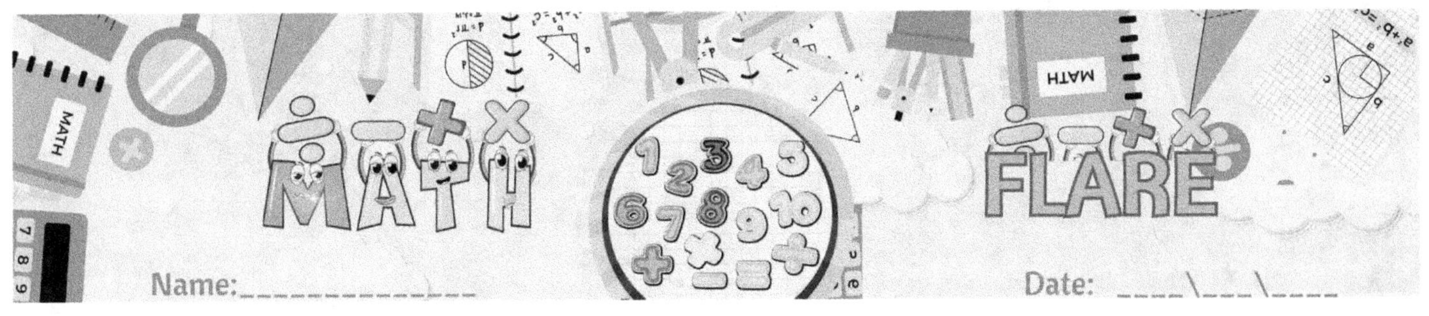

Compare the Fractions

Compare the fractions. Put the signs < , >, or =

220. $\dfrac{36}{38}$ ___ $\dfrac{27}{38}$

221. $\dfrac{26}{16}$ ___ $\dfrac{14}{16}$

222. $\dfrac{20}{80}$ ___ $\dfrac{165}{80}$

223. $\dfrac{20}{21}$ ___ $\dfrac{17}{21}$

224. $\dfrac{19}{30}$ ___ $\dfrac{18}{30}$

225. $\dfrac{7}{4}$ ___ $\dfrac{9}{4}$

226. $\dfrac{15}{6}$ ___ $\dfrac{1}{6}$

227. $\dfrac{10}{12}$ ___ $\dfrac{35}{12}$

228. $\dfrac{2}{5}$ ___ $\dfrac{8}{5}$

229. $\dfrac{39}{72}$ ___ $\dfrac{202}{72}$

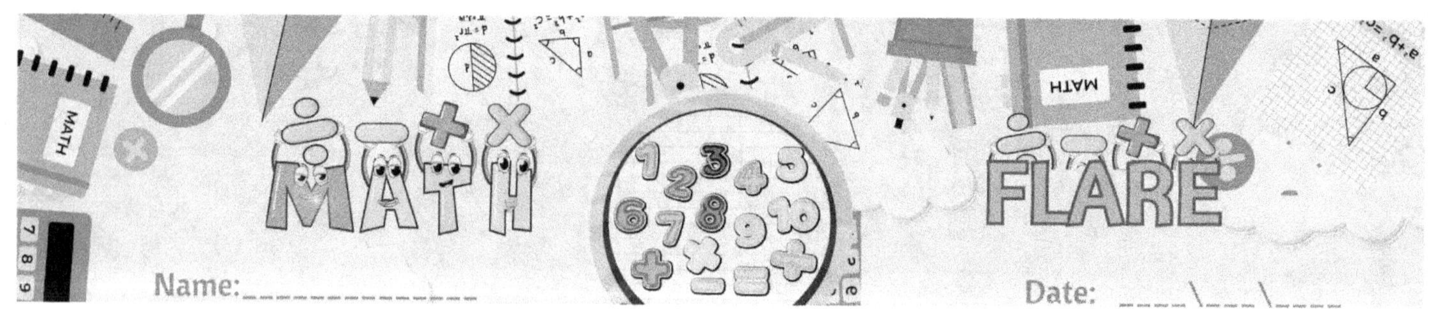

230. $\dfrac{22}{14}$ ___ $\dfrac{12}{14}$

231. $\dfrac{13}{25}$ ___ $\dfrac{20}{25}$

232. $\dfrac{2}{10}$ ___ $\dfrac{6}{10}$

233. $\dfrac{16}{17}$ ___ $\dfrac{30}{17}$

234. $\dfrac{7}{3}$ ___ $\dfrac{7}{3}$

235. $\dfrac{4}{9}$ ___ $\dfrac{1}{9}$

236. $\dfrac{30}{22}$ ___ $\dfrac{16}{22}$

237. $\dfrac{5}{2}$ ___ $\dfrac{1}{2}$

238. $\dfrac{44}{18}$ ___ $\dfrac{3}{18}$

239. $\dfrac{2}{7}$ ___ $\dfrac{9}{7}$

240. $\dfrac{45}{115}$ ___ $\dfrac{81}{115}$

241. $\dfrac{9}{24}$ ___ $\dfrac{27}{24}$

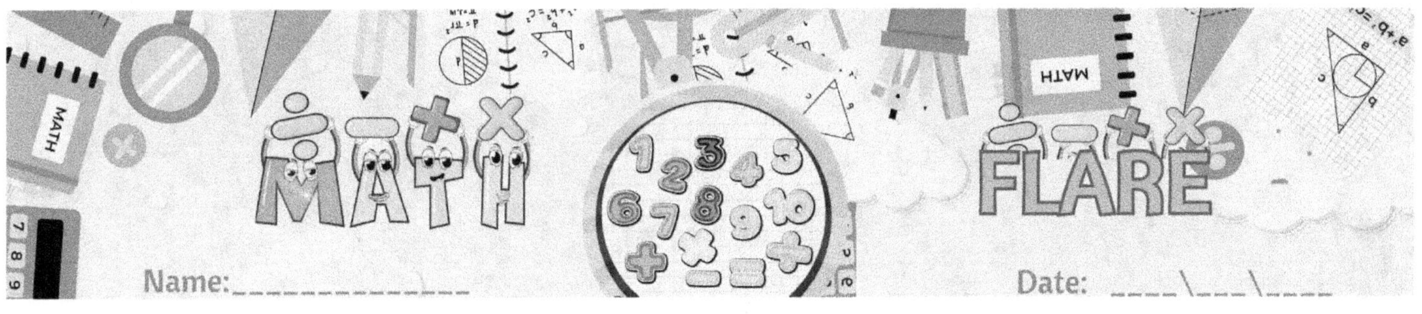

242. $\dfrac{36}{13}$ ___ $\dfrac{1}{13}$

243. $\dfrac{17}{15}$ ___ $\dfrac{6}{15}$

244. $\dfrac{35}{55}$ ___ $\dfrac{39}{55}$

245. $\dfrac{45}{57}$ ___ $\dfrac{32}{57}$

246. $\dfrac{11}{18}$ ___ $\dfrac{1}{18}$

247. $\dfrac{12}{20}$ ___ $\dfrac{14}{20}$

248. $\dfrac{7}{3}$ ___ $\dfrac{1}{3}$

249. $\dfrac{12}{10}$ ___ $\dfrac{6}{10}$

250. $\dfrac{40}{21}$ ___ $\dfrac{53}{21}$

251. $\dfrac{1}{2}$ ___ $\dfrac{3}{2}$

252. $\dfrac{11}{24}$ ___ $\dfrac{46}{24}$

253. $\dfrac{4}{16}$ ___ $\dfrac{10}{16}$

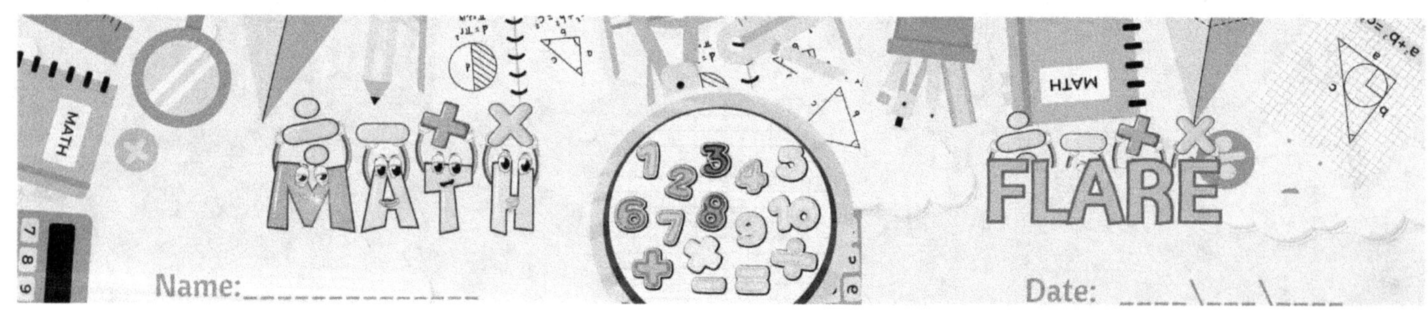

254. $\dfrac{2}{5}$ ___ $\dfrac{2}{5}$

255. $\dfrac{1}{22}$ ___ $\dfrac{14}{22}$

256. $\dfrac{2}{23}$ ___ $\dfrac{20}{23}$

257. $\dfrac{18}{7}$ ___ $\dfrac{16}{7}$

258. $\dfrac{55}{80}$ ___ $\dfrac{10}{80}$

259. $\dfrac{5}{6}$ ___ $\dfrac{1}{6}$

260. $\dfrac{5}{17}$ ___ $\dfrac{14}{17}$

261. $\dfrac{23}{8}$ ___ $\dfrac{1}{8}$

262. $\dfrac{36}{180}$ ___ $\dfrac{121}{180}$

263. $\dfrac{10}{18}$ ___ $\dfrac{16}{18}$

264. $\dfrac{2}{12}$ ___ $\dfrac{19}{12}$

265. $\dfrac{71}{25}$ ___ $\dfrac{32}{25}$

266. $\dfrac{6}{14}$ ___ $\dfrac{5}{14}$

267. $\dfrac{21}{45}$ ___ $\dfrac{39}{45}$

268. $\dfrac{9}{33}$ ___ $\dfrac{92}{33}$

269. $\dfrac{11}{4}$ ___ $\dfrac{3}{4}$

270. $\dfrac{12}{9}$ ___ $\dfrac{25}{9}$

271. $\dfrac{4}{24}$ ___ $\dfrac{10}{24}$

272. $\dfrac{23}{17}$ ___ $\dfrac{25}{17}$

273. $\dfrac{20}{32}$ ___ $\dfrac{14}{32}$

274. $\dfrac{3}{18}$ ___ $\dfrac{14}{18}$

275. $\dfrac{11}{6}$ ___ $\dfrac{14}{6}$

276. $\dfrac{20}{44}$ ___ $\dfrac{32}{44}$

277. $\dfrac{8}{20}$ ___ $\dfrac{58}{20}$

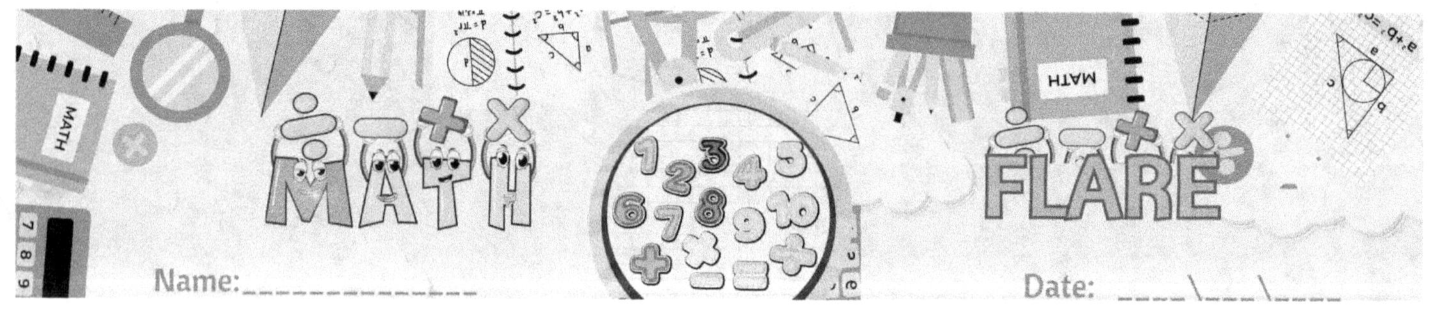

Equivalent Fractions

278. $\dfrac{6}{10} = \dfrac{}{40}$

279. $\dfrac{10}{15} = \dfrac{}{120}$

280. $\dfrac{1}{3} = \dfrac{}{12}$

281. $\dfrac{}{7} = \dfrac{10}{35}$

282. $\dfrac{1}{} = \dfrac{6}{48}$

283. $\dfrac{2}{} = \dfrac{6}{27}$

284. $\dfrac{3}{4} = \dfrac{}{32}$

285. $\dfrac{11}{} = \dfrac{55}{65}$

286. $\dfrac{}{2} = \dfrac{5}{10}$

287. $\dfrac{}{18} = \dfrac{54}{162}$

Name:_________________   Date: ______________

288. $\dfrac{8}{13} = \dfrac{32}{}$

289. $\dfrac{1}{} = \dfrac{3}{12}$

290. $\dfrac{14}{19} = \dfrac{}{76}$

291. $\dfrac{3}{} = \dfrac{24}{48}$

292. $\dfrac{6}{7} = \dfrac{}{14}$

293. $\dfrac{13}{20} = \dfrac{}{180}$

294. $\dfrac{4}{5} = \dfrac{8}{}$

295. $\dfrac{}{17} = \dfrac{42}{51}$

296. $\dfrac{9}{} = \dfrac{81}{99}$

297. $\dfrac{1}{2} = \dfrac{6}{}$

298. $\dfrac{8}{} = \dfrac{24}{54}$

299. $\dfrac{3}{14} = \dfrac{24}{}$

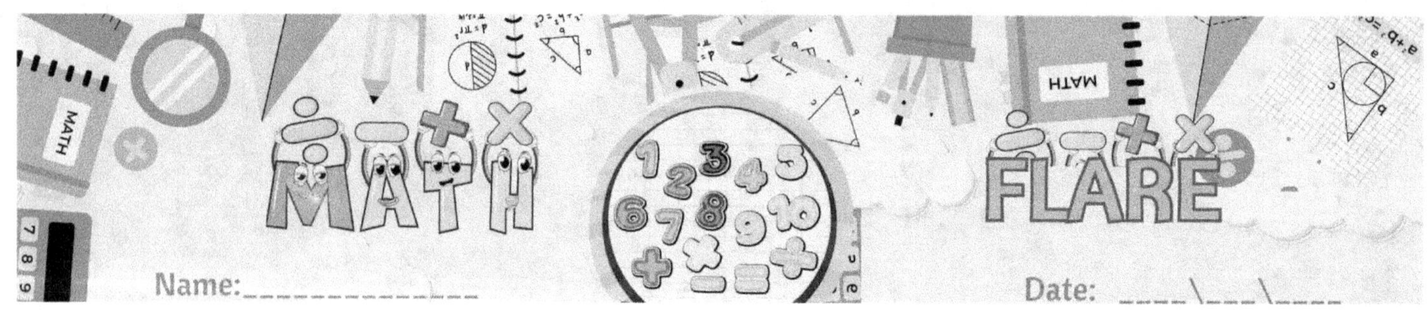

300. $\dfrac{}{12} = \dfrac{25}{60}$

301. $\dfrac{}{8} = \dfrac{48}{64}$

302. $\dfrac{4}{} = \dfrac{40}{100}$

303. $\dfrac{}{9} = \dfrac{32}{72}$

304. $\dfrac{}{16} = \dfrac{80}{128}$

305. $\dfrac{6}{15} = \dfrac{}{30}$

306. $\dfrac{}{3} = \dfrac{8}{12}$

307. $\dfrac{7}{11} = \dfrac{42}{}$

308. $\dfrac{4}{} = \dfrac{24}{84}$

309. $\dfrac{6}{15} = \dfrac{}{45}$

310. $\dfrac{5}{} = \dfrac{50}{200}$

311. $\dfrac{1}{2} = \dfrac{}{18}$

312. $\dfrac{}{3} = \dfrac{4}{6}$

313. $\dfrac{11}{} = \dfrac{88}{136}$

314. $\dfrac{3}{} = \dfrac{12}{52}$

315. $\dfrac{2}{8} = \dfrac{6}{}$

316. $\dfrac{6}{16} = \dfrac{48}{}$

317. $\dfrac{}{4} = \dfrac{12}{24}$

318. $\dfrac{13}{18} = \dfrac{}{180}$

319. $\dfrac{3}{5} = \dfrac{27}{}$

320. $\dfrac{}{10} = \dfrac{30}{60}$

321. $\dfrac{}{7} = \dfrac{9}{21}$

322. $\dfrac{2}{} = \dfrac{12}{36}$

323. $\dfrac{4}{12} = \dfrac{}{36}$

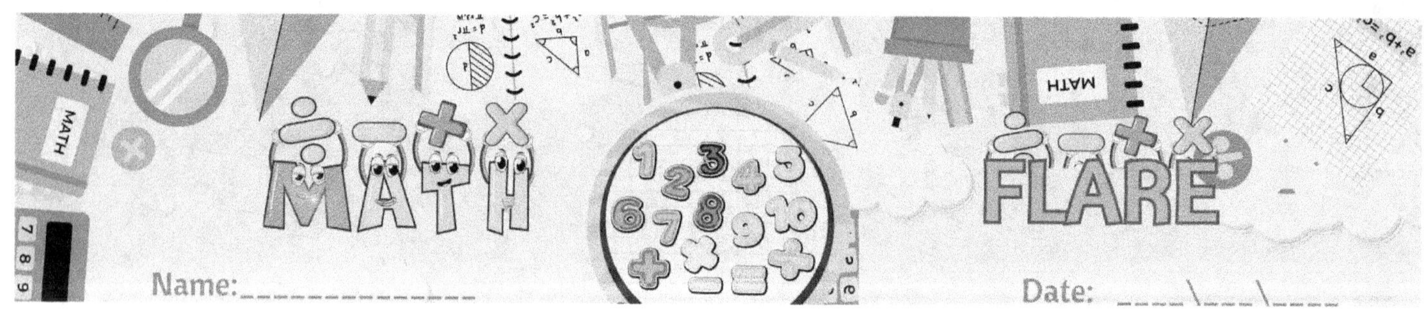

324. $\dfrac{}{9} = \dfrac{20}{36}$

325. $\dfrac{7}{19} = \dfrac{35}{}$

326. $\dfrac{5}{} = \dfrac{45}{54}$

327. $\dfrac{6}{8} = \dfrac{}{32}$

328. $\dfrac{}{20} = \dfrac{65}{100}$

329. $\dfrac{8}{11} = \dfrac{40}{}$

330. $\dfrac{1}{} = \dfrac{4}{72}$

331. $\dfrac{8}{15} = \dfrac{48}{}$

332. $\dfrac{8}{19} = \dfrac{48}{}$

333. $\dfrac{1}{4} = \dfrac{5}{}$

334. $\dfrac{1}{2} = \dfrac{}{14}$

335. $\dfrac{14}{16} = \dfrac{}{96}$

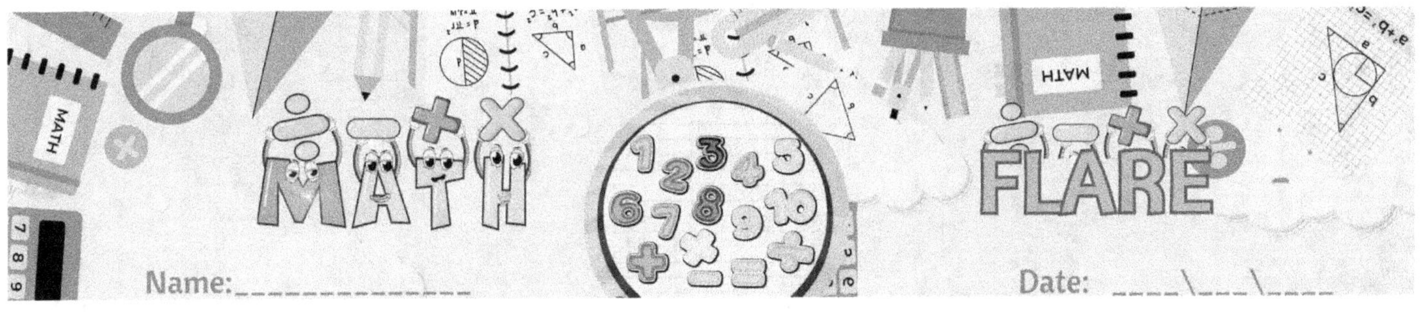

Fractions Addition: Common Denominator

Find the sum.

336. $\dfrac{1}{4} + \dfrac{1}{4} =$ _____________

337. $\dfrac{2}{5} + \dfrac{2}{5} =$ _____________

338. $\dfrac{1}{3} + \dfrac{1}{3} =$ _____________

339. $\dfrac{1}{7} + \dfrac{5}{7} =$ _____________

340. $\dfrac{3}{11} + \dfrac{6}{11} =$ _____________

341. $\dfrac{2}{6} + \dfrac{3}{6} =$ _____________

342. $\dfrac{1}{2} + \dfrac{1}{2} =$ _____________

343. $\dfrac{5}{9} + \dfrac{2}{9} =$ _____________

344. $\dfrac{2}{12} + \dfrac{2}{12} =$ _____________

345. $\dfrac{1}{8} + \dfrac{5}{8} =$ _____________

346. $\dfrac{6}{10} + \dfrac{1}{10} =$ _____________

347. $\dfrac{3}{5} + \dfrac{1}{5} =$ _____________

348. $\dfrac{2}{4} + \dfrac{1}{4} =$ _______________

349. $\dfrac{3}{6} + \dfrac{1}{6} =$ _______________

350. $\dfrac{2}{11} + \dfrac{3}{11} =$ _______________

351. $\dfrac{4}{12} + \dfrac{2}{12} =$ _______________

352. $\dfrac{1}{7} + \dfrac{1}{7} =$ _______________

353. $\dfrac{3}{7} + \dfrac{2}{7} =$ _______________

354. $\dfrac{5}{9} + \dfrac{3}{9} =$ _______________

355. $\dfrac{3}{10} + \dfrac{5}{10} =$ _______________

356. $\dfrac{2}{8} + \dfrac{4}{8} =$ _______________

357. $\dfrac{2}{5} + \dfrac{1}{5} =$ _______________

358. $\dfrac{1}{12} + \dfrac{2}{12} =$ _______________

359. $\dfrac{1}{11} + \dfrac{8}{11} =$ _______________

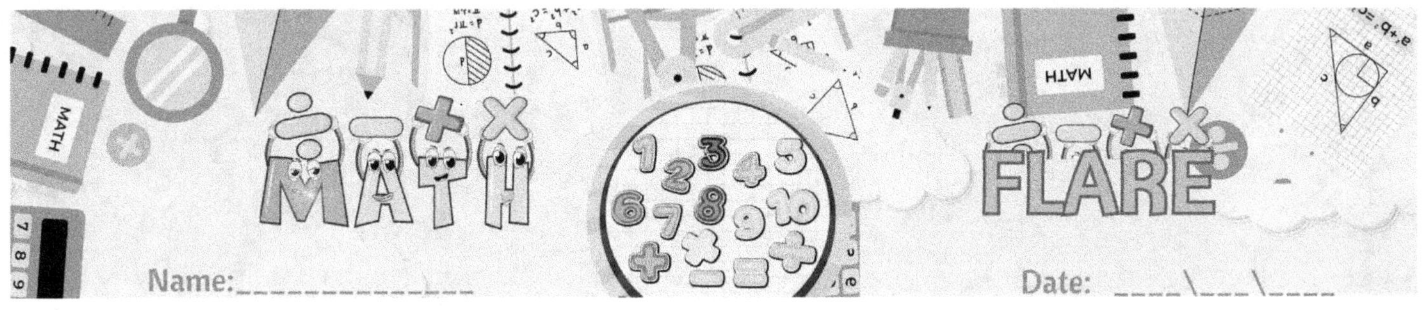

360. $\dfrac{1}{4} + \dfrac{2}{4} =$ _______________

361. $\dfrac{2}{8} + \dfrac{1}{8} =$ _______________

362. $\dfrac{1}{11} + \dfrac{6}{11} =$ _______________

363. $\dfrac{1}{10} + \dfrac{8}{10} =$ _______________

364. $\dfrac{1}{9} + \dfrac{1}{9} =$ _______________

365. $\dfrac{2}{12} + \dfrac{3}{12} =$ _______________

366. $\dfrac{1}{7} + \dfrac{3}{7} =$ _______________

367. $\dfrac{1}{6} + \dfrac{1}{6} =$ _______________

368. $\dfrac{1}{5} + \dfrac{1}{5} =$ _______________

369. $\dfrac{1}{6} + \dfrac{3}{6} =$ _______________

370. $\dfrac{7}{10} + \dfrac{1}{10} =$ _______________

371. $\dfrac{7}{11} + \dfrac{2}{11} =$ _______________

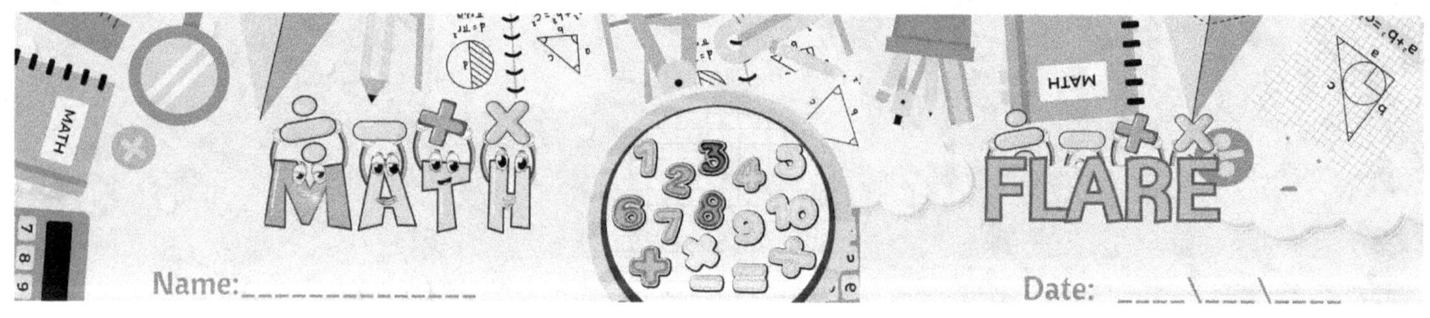

372. $\dfrac{1}{8} + \dfrac{1}{8} =$ _______________

373. $\dfrac{1}{12} + \dfrac{3}{12} =$ _______________

374. $\dfrac{1}{5} + \dfrac{2}{5} =$ _______________

375. $\dfrac{4}{7} + \dfrac{2}{7} =$ _______________

376. $\dfrac{6}{9} + \dfrac{2}{9} =$ _______________

377. $\dfrac{4}{6} + \dfrac{1}{6} =$ _______________

378. $\dfrac{1}{11} + \dfrac{9}{11} =$ _______________

379. $\dfrac{3}{9} + \dfrac{2}{9} =$ _______________

380. $\dfrac{2}{12} + \dfrac{9}{12} =$ _______________

381. $\dfrac{5}{10} + \dfrac{1}{10} =$ _______________

382. $\dfrac{1}{8} + \dfrac{3}{8} =$ _______________

383. $\dfrac{3}{7} + \dfrac{3}{7} =$ _______________

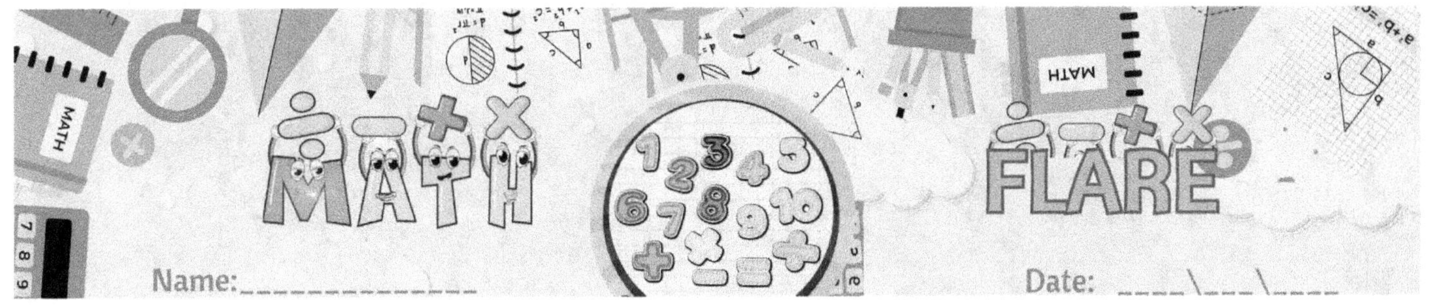

384. $\dfrac{2}{12} + \dfrac{1}{12} =$ _______________

385. $\dfrac{3}{11} + \dfrac{4}{11} =$ _______________

386. $\dfrac{1}{5} + \dfrac{3}{5} =$ _______________

387. $\dfrac{2}{6} + \dfrac{1}{6} =$ _______________

388. $\dfrac{1}{8} + \dfrac{6}{8} =$ _______________

389. $\dfrac{2}{10} + \dfrac{1}{10} =$ _______________

390. $\dfrac{4}{11} + \dfrac{5}{11} =$ _______________

391. $\dfrac{4}{10} + \dfrac{5}{10} =$ _______________

392. $\dfrac{3}{6} + \dfrac{2}{6} =$ _______________

393. $\dfrac{4}{9} + \dfrac{1}{9} =$ _______________

394. $\dfrac{4}{7} + \dfrac{1}{7} =$ _______________

395. $\dfrac{1}{8} + \dfrac{4}{8} =$ _______________

Fractions Subtraction - Common Denominator

Find the difference.

396. $\dfrac{8}{11} - \dfrac{5}{11} =$ _______________

397. $\dfrac{4}{6} - \dfrac{1}{6} =$ _______________

398. $\dfrac{7}{9} - \dfrac{5}{9} =$ _______________

399. $\dfrac{5}{7} - \dfrac{4}{7} =$ _______________

400. $\dfrac{2}{3} - \dfrac{1}{3} =$ _______________

401. $\dfrac{3}{5} - \dfrac{2}{5} =$ _______________

402. $\dfrac{9}{12} - \dfrac{8}{12} =$ _______________

403. $\dfrac{3}{4} - \dfrac{2}{4} =$ _______________

404. $\dfrac{6}{10} - \dfrac{1}{10} =$ _______________

405. $\dfrac{8}{9} - \dfrac{2}{9} =$ _______________

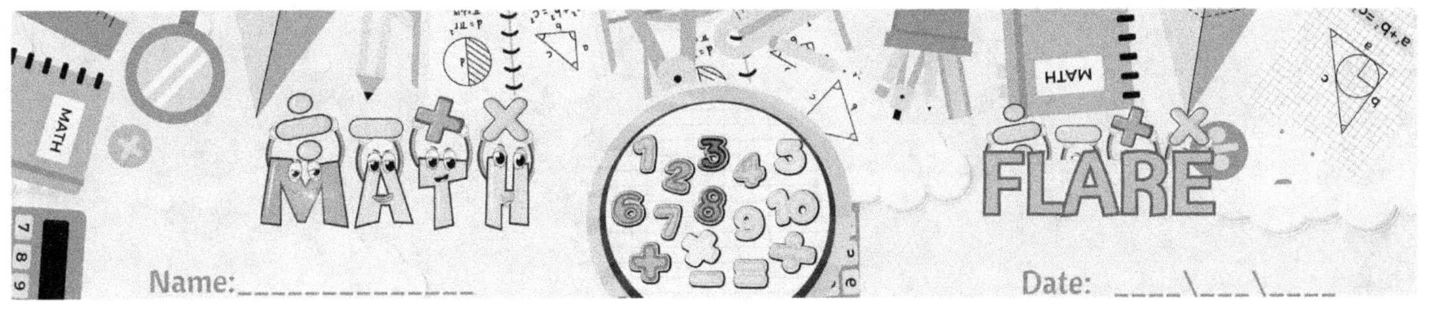

406. $\dfrac{4}{11} - \dfrac{1}{11} =$ _____________

407. $\dfrac{5}{6} - \dfrac{4}{6} =$ _____________

408. $\dfrac{6}{7} - \dfrac{5}{7} =$ _____________

409. $\dfrac{6}{12} - \dfrac{5}{12} =$ _____________

410. $\dfrac{8}{10} - \dfrac{4}{10} =$ _____________

411. $\dfrac{6}{8} - \dfrac{4}{8} =$ _____________

412. $\dfrac{6}{8} - \dfrac{5}{8} =$ _____________

413. $\dfrac{3}{9} - \dfrac{1}{9} =$ _____________

414. $\dfrac{9}{11} - \dfrac{6}{11} =$ _____________

415. $\dfrac{5}{6} - \dfrac{2}{6} =$ _____________

416. $\dfrac{11}{12} - \dfrac{10}{12} =$ _____________

417. $\dfrac{2}{5} - \dfrac{1}{5} =$ _____________

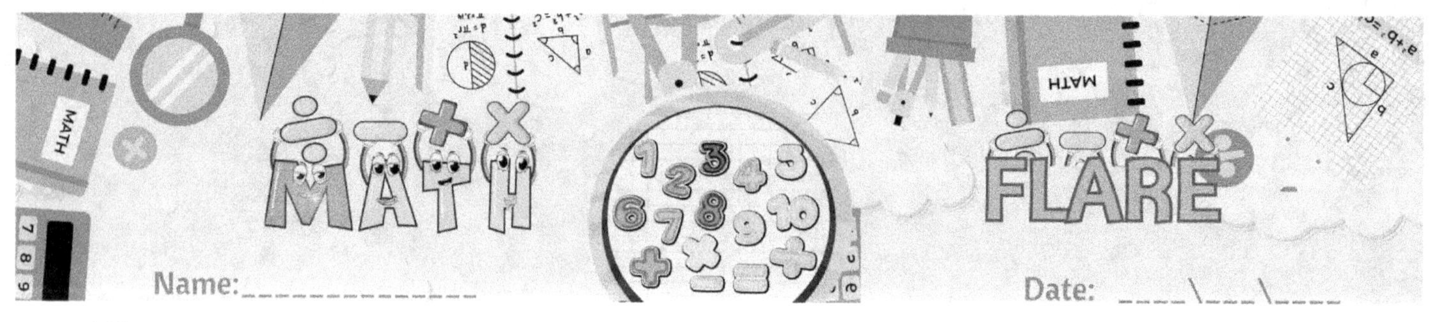

418. $\dfrac{4}{7} - \dfrac{3}{7} =$ _______________

419. $\dfrac{9}{10} - \dfrac{5}{10} =$ _______________

420. $\dfrac{6}{7} - \dfrac{4}{7} =$ _______________

421. $\dfrac{9}{11} - \dfrac{1}{11} =$ _______________

422. $\dfrac{9}{12} - \dfrac{5}{12} =$ _______________

423. $\dfrac{7}{10} - \dfrac{6}{10} =$ _______________

424. $\dfrac{2}{4} - \dfrac{1}{4} =$ _______________

425. $\dfrac{8}{9} - \dfrac{6}{9} =$ _______________

426. $\dfrac{6}{7} - \dfrac{1}{7} =$ _______________

427. $\dfrac{3}{10} - \dfrac{2}{10} =$ _______________

428. $\dfrac{3}{6} - \dfrac{1}{6} =$ _______________

429. $\dfrac{10}{11} - \dfrac{9}{11} =$ _______________

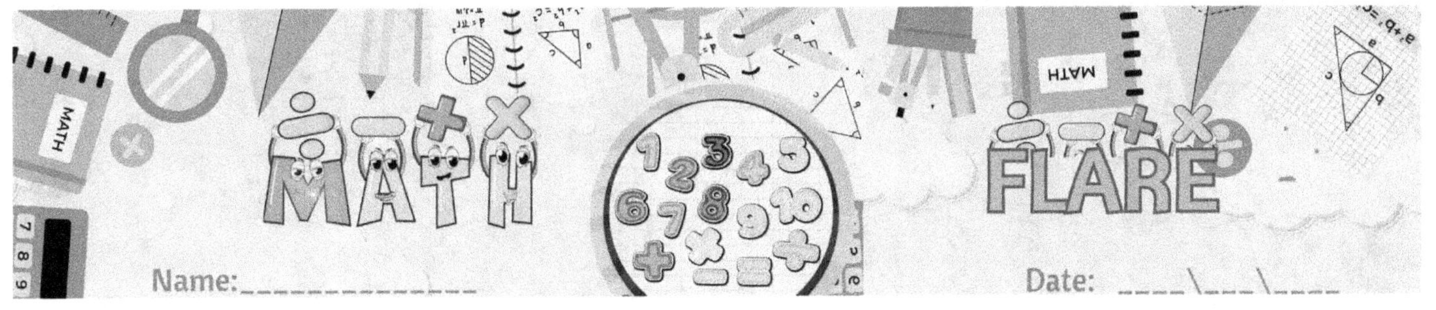

430. $\dfrac{7}{9} - \dfrac{1}{9} =$ _______________

431. $\dfrac{10}{12} - \dfrac{2}{12} =$ _______________

432. $\dfrac{6}{8} - \dfrac{1}{8} =$ _______________

433. $\dfrac{8}{11} - \dfrac{1}{11} =$ _______________

434. $\dfrac{7}{8} - \dfrac{6}{8} =$ _______________

435. $\dfrac{3}{4} - \dfrac{1}{4} =$ _______________

436. $\dfrac{4}{5} - \dfrac{2}{5} =$ _______________

437. $\dfrac{8}{9} - \dfrac{7}{9} =$ _______________

438. $\dfrac{9}{10} - \dfrac{4}{10} =$ _______________

439. $\dfrac{6}{7} - \dfrac{3}{7} =$ _______________

440. $\dfrac{8}{12} - \dfrac{7}{12} =$ _______________

441. $\dfrac{3}{7} - \dfrac{2}{7} =$ _______________

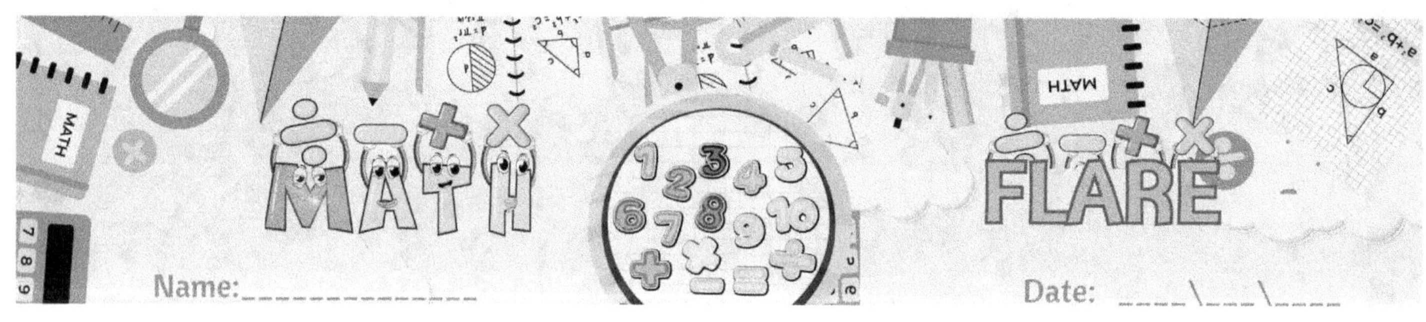

442. $\dfrac{8}{12} - \dfrac{4}{12} =$ _______________

443. $\dfrac{3}{6} - \dfrac{2}{6} =$ _______________

444. $\dfrac{4}{10} - \dfrac{2}{10} =$ _______________

445. $\dfrac{3}{8} - \dfrac{2}{8} =$ _______________

446. $\dfrac{10}{12} - \dfrac{9}{12} =$ _______________

447. $\dfrac{6}{11} - \dfrac{2}{11} =$ _______________

448. $\dfrac{6}{9} - \dfrac{4}{9} =$ _______________

449. $\dfrac{4}{6} - \dfrac{3}{6} =$ _______________

450. $\dfrac{4}{8} - \dfrac{1}{8} =$ _______________

451. $\dfrac{4}{5} - \dfrac{3}{5} =$ _______________

452. $\dfrac{2}{6} - \dfrac{1}{6} =$ _______________

453. $\dfrac{10}{12} - \dfrac{7}{12} =$ _______________

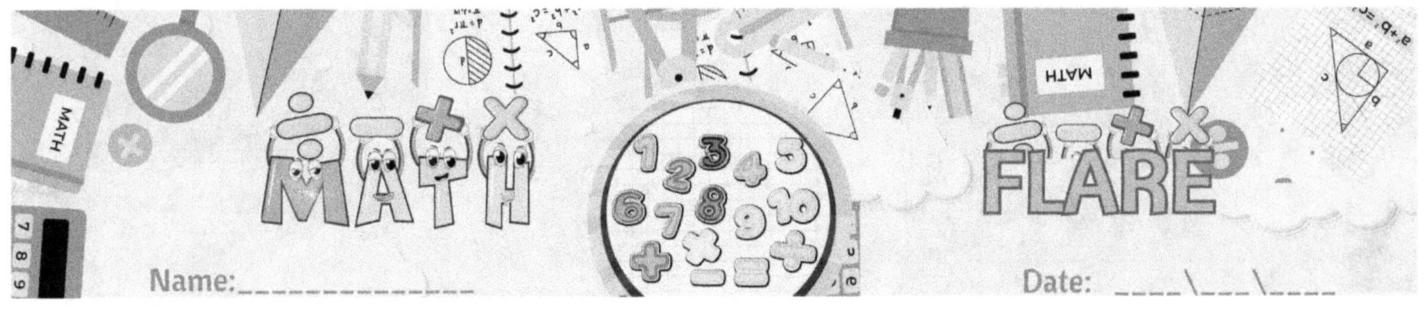

Fractions Multiplication

Find the product.

454. $\dfrac{9}{11} \times \dfrac{2}{3} =$ ___________________

455. $\dfrac{7}{8} \times \dfrac{5}{7} =$ ___________________

456. $\dfrac{1}{2} \times \dfrac{1}{16} =$ ___________________

457. $\dfrac{10}{13} \times \dfrac{5}{7} =$ ___________________

458. $\dfrac{1}{2} \times \dfrac{7}{12} =$ ___________________

459. $\dfrac{2}{3} \times \dfrac{1}{2} =$ ___________________

460. $\dfrac{3}{5} \times \dfrac{1}{2} =$ ___________________

461. $\dfrac{4}{5} \times \dfrac{5}{14} =$ ___________________

462. $\dfrac{9}{11} \times \dfrac{1}{5} =$ ___________________

463. $\dfrac{8}{13} \times \dfrac{8}{9} =$ ___________________

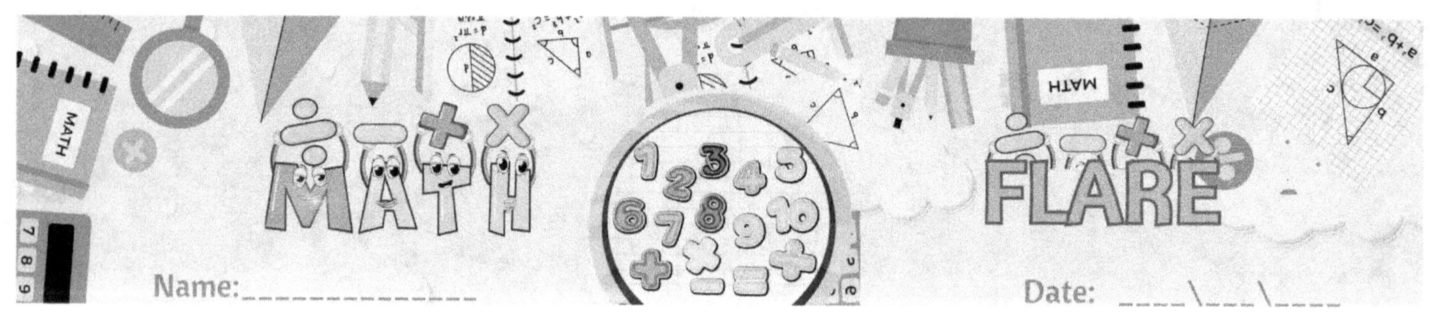

464. $\dfrac{1}{7} \times \dfrac{3}{4} =$ _______________

465. $\dfrac{1}{2} \times \dfrac{4}{5} =$ _______________

466. $\dfrac{7}{10} \times \dfrac{11}{16} =$ _______________

467. $\dfrac{1}{2} \times \dfrac{1}{3} =$ _______________

468. $\dfrac{1}{5} \times \dfrac{3}{5} =$ _______________

469. $\dfrac{3}{8} \times \dfrac{5}{6} =$ _______________

470. $\dfrac{3}{5} \times \dfrac{2}{3} =$ _______________

471. $\dfrac{1}{4} \times \dfrac{1}{2} =$ _______________

472. $\dfrac{7}{12} \times \dfrac{4}{5} =$ _______________

473. $\dfrac{8}{11} \times \dfrac{9}{14} =$ _______________

474. $\dfrac{1}{2} \times \dfrac{1}{2} =$ _______________

475. $\dfrac{5}{12} \times \dfrac{7}{8} =$ _______________

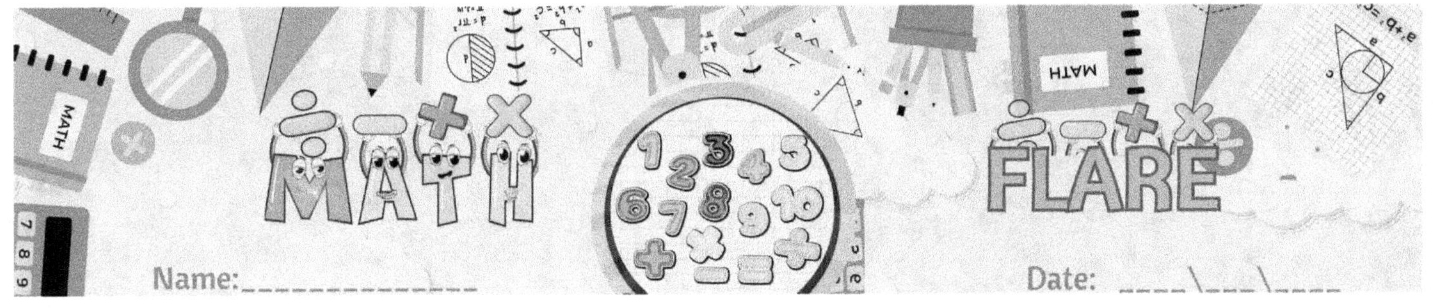

Name: ___________________ Date: _____ __________

476. $\dfrac{3}{8} \times \dfrac{3}{10} =$ _________________

477. $\dfrac{3}{10} \times \dfrac{1}{3} =$ _________________

478. $\dfrac{6}{7} \times \dfrac{5}{7} =$ _________________

479. $\dfrac{1}{5} \times \dfrac{1}{3} =$ _________________

480. $\dfrac{5}{11} \times \dfrac{3}{4} =$ _________________

481. $\dfrac{2}{5} \times \dfrac{1}{6} =$ _________________

482. $\dfrac{1}{2} \times \dfrac{1}{8} =$ _________________

483. $\dfrac{15}{16} \times \dfrac{2}{3} =$ _________________

484. $\dfrac{3}{4} \times \dfrac{3}{5} =$ _________________

485. $\dfrac{7}{12} \times \dfrac{7}{13} =$ _________________

486. $\dfrac{1}{3} \times \dfrac{3}{4} =$ _________________

487. $\dfrac{8}{9} \times \dfrac{14}{15} =$ _________________

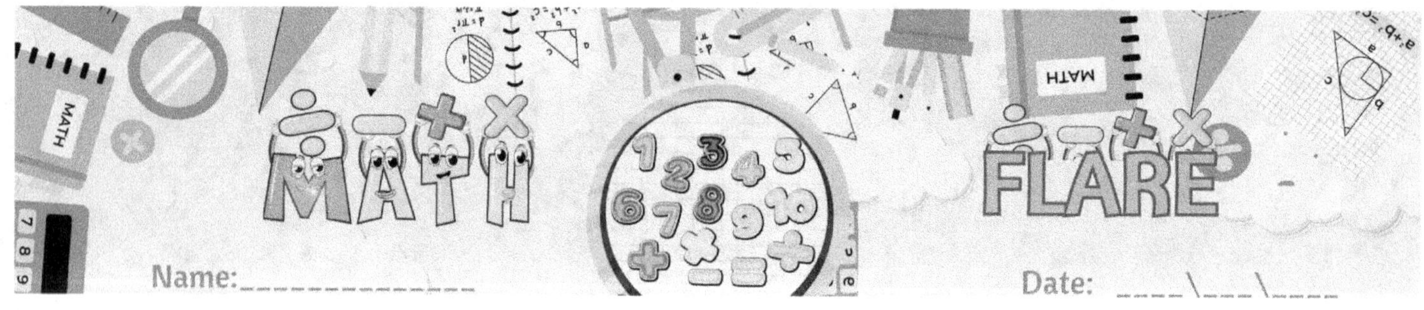

Fractions Division

Find the quotient.

488. $\dfrac{1}{2} \div \dfrac{3}{6} =$ ___________

489. $\dfrac{3}{4} \div \dfrac{1}{11} =$ ___________

490. $\dfrac{2}{9} \div \dfrac{8}{9} =$ ___________

491. $\dfrac{5}{12} \div \dfrac{9}{12} =$ ___________

492. $\dfrac{3}{10} \div \dfrac{5}{8} =$ ___________

493. $\dfrac{1}{2} \div \dfrac{3}{7} =$ ___________

494. $\dfrac{3}{8} \div \dfrac{1}{7} =$ ___________

495. $\dfrac{1}{5} \div \dfrac{5}{11} =$ ___________

496. $\dfrac{1}{6} \div \dfrac{2}{9} =$ ___________

497. $\dfrac{1}{4} \div \dfrac{4}{5} =$ ___________

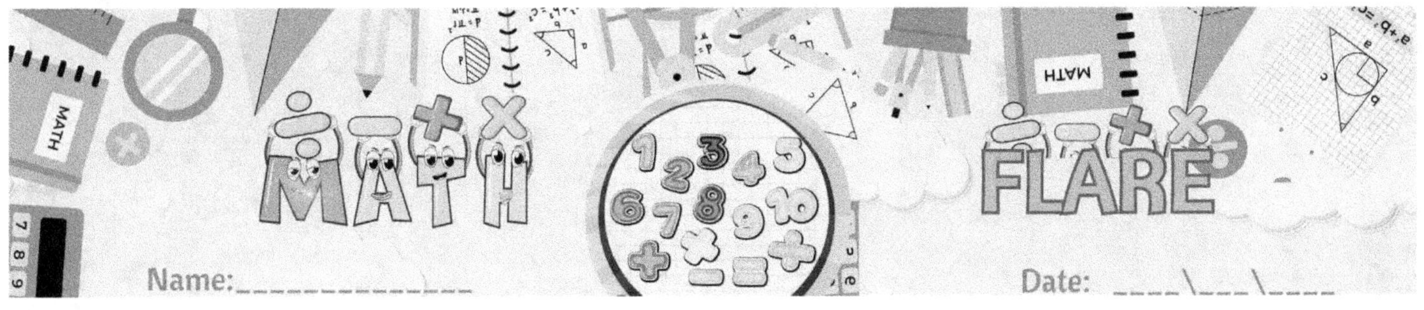

498. $\dfrac{2}{7} \div \dfrac{2}{10} =$ _______________

499. $\dfrac{3}{10} \div \dfrac{6}{12} =$ _______________

500. $\dfrac{2}{3} \div \dfrac{8}{9} =$ _______________

501. $\dfrac{6}{7} \div \dfrac{1}{2} =$ _______________

502. $\dfrac{8}{11} \div \dfrac{9}{10} =$ _______________

503. $\dfrac{1}{2} \div \dfrac{4}{7} =$ _______________

504. $\dfrac{3}{8} \div \dfrac{2}{6} =$ _______________

505. $\dfrac{1}{10} \div \dfrac{4}{9} =$ _______________

506. $\dfrac{2}{3} \div \dfrac{2}{8} =$ _______________

507. $\dfrac{9}{11} \div \dfrac{3}{7} =$ _______________

508. $\dfrac{1}{8} \div \dfrac{2}{4} =$ _______________

509. $\dfrac{3}{5} \div \dfrac{3}{5} =$ _______________

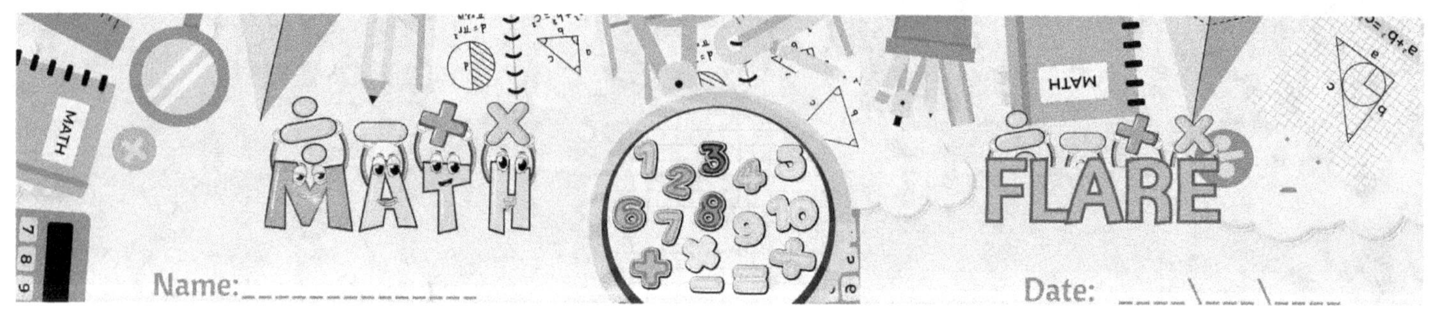

510. $\dfrac{1}{6} \div \dfrac{1}{2} =$ _______________

511. $\dfrac{1}{3} \div \dfrac{2}{3} =$ _______________

512. $\dfrac{4}{7} \div \dfrac{1}{9} =$ _______________

513. $\dfrac{1}{2} \div \dfrac{1}{8} =$ _______________

514. $\dfrac{2}{5} \div \dfrac{1}{4} =$ _______________

515. $\dfrac{5}{8} \div \dfrac{4}{5} =$ _______________

516. $\dfrac{1}{6} \div \dfrac{4}{12} =$ _______________

517. $\dfrac{1}{2} \div \dfrac{3}{8} =$ _______________

518. $\dfrac{1}{7} \div \dfrac{1}{2} =$ _______________

519. $\dfrac{7}{8} \div \dfrac{3}{6} =$ _______________

520. $\dfrac{9}{10} \div \dfrac{2}{3} =$ _______________

521. $\dfrac{1}{11} \div \dfrac{1}{7} =$ _______________

Fractions Addition Word Problems

522. Leah baked $\frac{6}{10}$ of her cakes for her friends and then kept $\frac{2}{8}$ of them for herself. How many cakes did she bake in total?

523. Samuel drank $\frac{1}{2}$ of a bottle of water and then drank another $\frac{1}{5}$ of the bottle later. How much of the bottle did he drink in total?

524. Grace used $\frac{1}{3}$ of a container of milk in a recipe and then used another $\frac{1}{3}$ of the container in a different recipe. How much of the container did she use in total?

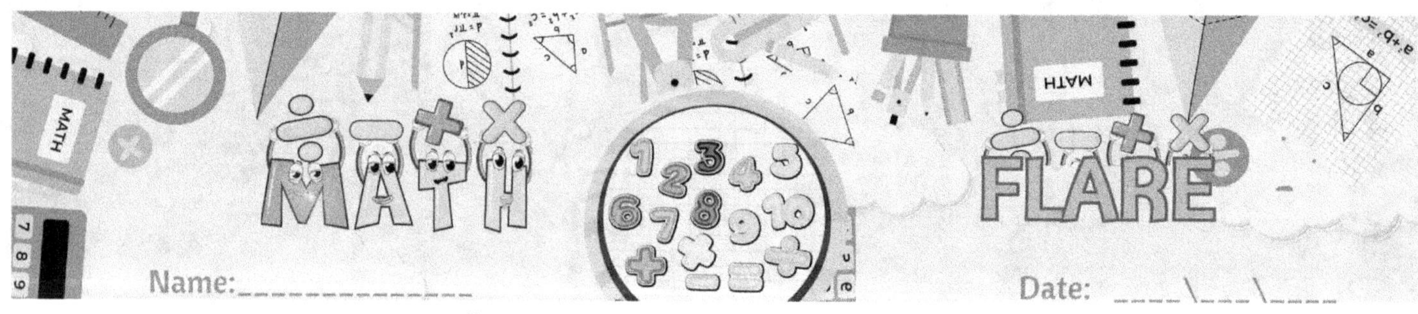

525. Kinsley extracts $\frac{5}{8}$ of a glass of orange juice and then added $\frac{1}{7}$ of a glass of apple juice. How much juice is in the glass in total?

526. What is $\frac{2}{6}$ plus $\frac{4}{8}$?

527. A recipe calls for $\frac{2}{5}$ cups of flour and $\frac{3}{7}$ cups of tomato sauce. How much of the ingredients are needed in total for the recipe?

528. A recipe calls for $\frac{5}{9}$ cups of milk and $\frac{2}{5}$ cups of cream. How much liquid in total is needed for the recipe?

529. Ryder spent $\frac{2}{5}$ of his allowance on a phones and then spent another $\frac{1}{3}$ of his allowance on a video game. How much money did he spend in total?

530. Molly walked $\frac{1}{4}$ miles to the store and then walked back home another $\frac{1}{6}$ miles. How far did she walk in total?

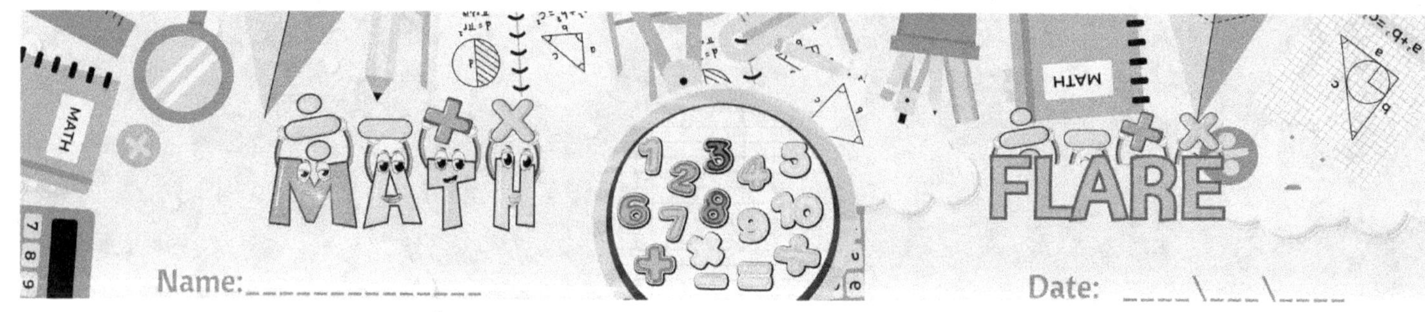

531. Claire bought $\frac{4}{8}$ of a pound of ground beef and then added another $\frac{4}{10}$ of a pound to make a hamburger patty. How much ground beef did she use in total?

532. Everly made a salad with $\frac{3}{6}$ of a cup of lettuce and $\frac{1}{6}$ of a cup of spinach. How much salad did she make in total?

533. A car travels $\frac{3}{5}$ of a mile at a constant speed and then travels another $\frac{2}{7}$ of a mile at a different constant speed. How far did the car travel in total?

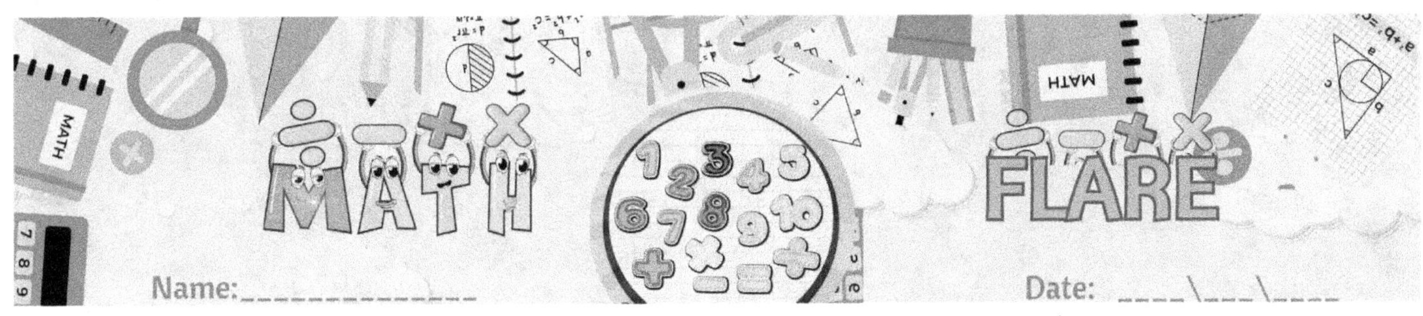

534. Nolan ate $\frac{2}{4}$ of his pizza for dinner and then ate $\frac{1}{5}$ of the leftovers for lunch the next day. How much of his pizza did he eat in total?

535. Liam walked $\frac{4}{7}$ of a mile to the store and then walked another $\frac{2}{9}$ of a mile back home. How far did he walk in total?

536. Aiden drank $\frac{1}{2}$ of a bottle of juice and then drank another $\frac{1}{3}$ of the bottle later. How much of the bottle did he drink in total?

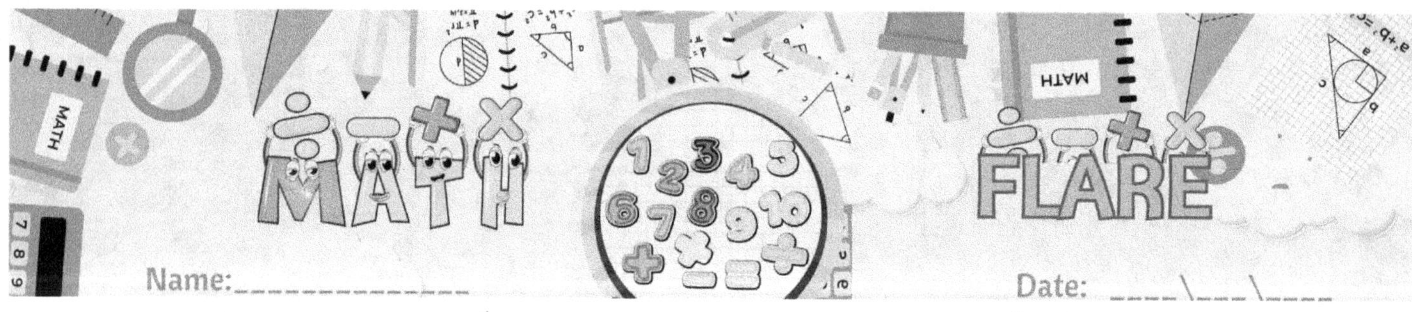

Name:_________________   Date: ____________

537. A recipe calls for $\frac{1}{6}$ cups of peanut butter and $\frac{2}{8}$ cups of jelly. How much of the ingredients are needed in total for the recipe?

538. Lincoln mixed $\frac{2}{3}$ of a cup of milk and $\frac{1}{4}$ of a cup of water in his morning drink. How much liquid did he use in total?

539. Penelope cycled $\frac{1}{2}$ miles. She then stopped to buy some groceries. Then she cycled $\frac{2}{7}$ more miles. How far did Penelope cycle in total?

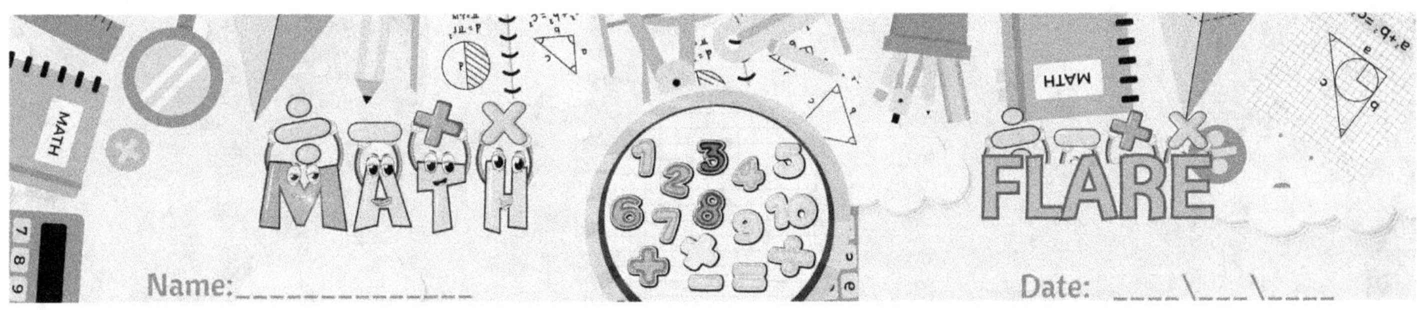

540. Ethan ran $\frac{1}{4}$ of a mile and then walked another $\frac{4}{6}$ of a mile. How far did he travel in total?

541. Jordan drove $\frac{1}{10}$ of a mile and then walked $\frac{3}{5}$ of a mile to his friend's house. How far did he travel in total?

542. A recipe calls for $\frac{1}{2}$ cups of sugar and $\frac{3}{7}$ cups of flour. How much of the mixture is needed in total?

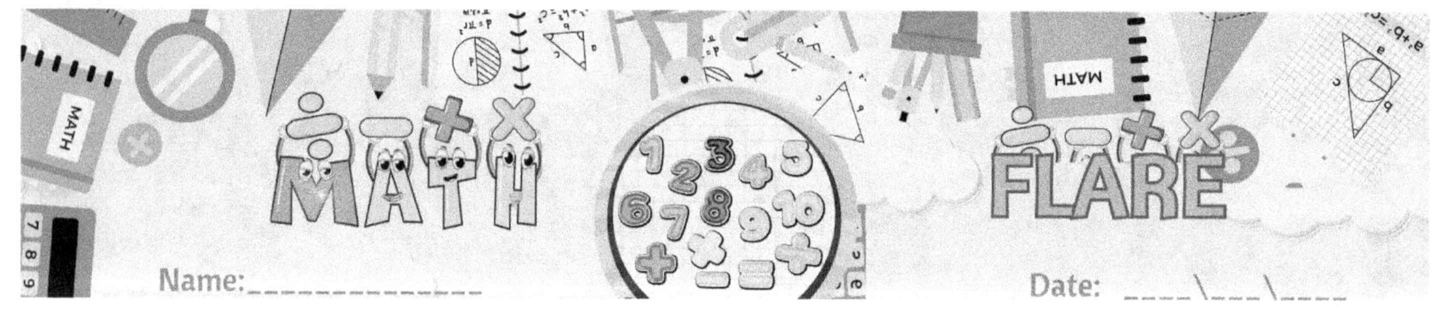

Fractions Subtraction Word Problems

543. Maya is running on a track that is $\frac{2}{4}$ of a mile long. She has already run $\frac{2}{5}$ of the mile. How much further does she have to run?

544. Peyton has a book that is $\frac{7}{8}$ of an inch thick. She reads $\frac{1}{4}$ of the book. How thick is the remaining portion of the book in inches?

545. Diego has a length of ribbon that is $\frac{1}{2}$ meters long. He wants to cut off $\frac{4}{10}$ of the ribbon to use for a gift. How long will the remaining ribbon be?

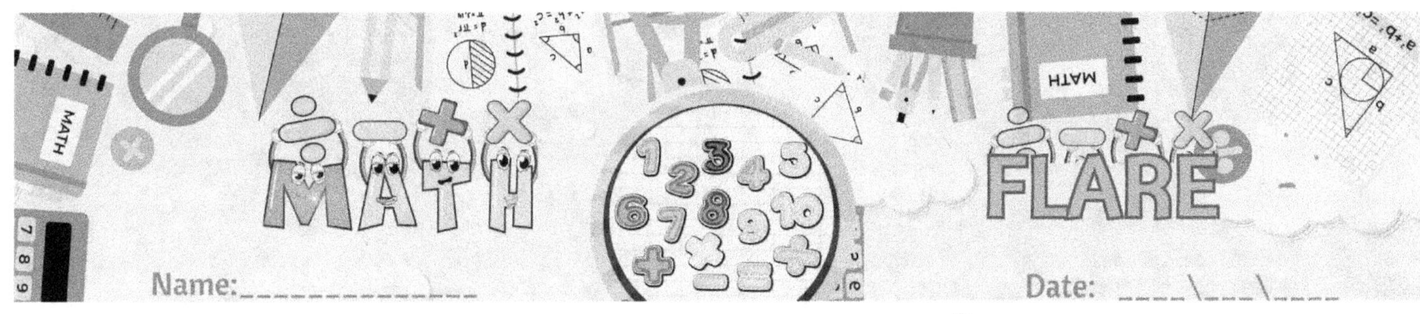

546. Colton is making a sandwich that calls for $\frac{2}{3}$ of a pound of beef. He only has $\frac{1}{2}$ of a pound of beef left. How much more beef does he need to make the sandwich?

547. Gabriella has $\frac{5}{6}$ of a pound of ground chicken. She uses $\frac{1}{3}$ of the chicken to make a burger. How much chicken is left in pounds?

548. A container has $\frac{3}{8}$ of a gallon of milk. If $\frac{1}{4}$ of the milk is taken out and put into another container, how much milk is left in the original container in gallons?

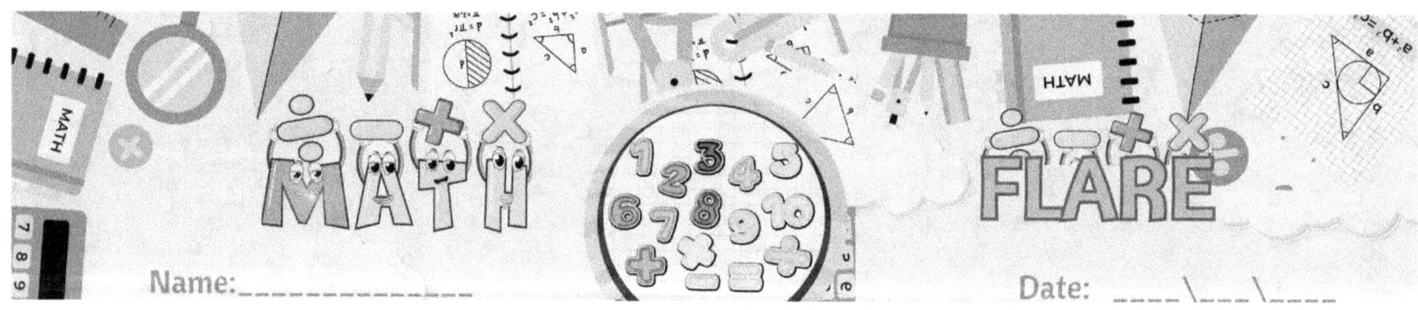

549. A recipe calls for $\frac{4}{10}$ of a cup of sugar. If $\frac{3}{8}$ of the sugar is already used, how much sugar is left in cups?

550. Liam has $\frac{7}{8}$ of a liter of juice. He drinks $\frac{3}{7}$ of the juice. How much juice is left in liters?

551. Isabelle wants to make a dish that calls for $\frac{1}{2}$ of a cup of yogurt. She only has $\frac{1}{6}$ of a cup of yogurt left. How much more yogurt does she need to make the dish?

552. Kai has $\frac{5}{9}$ of a pound of cheese. He uses $\frac{2}{5}$ of the cheese to make a sandwich. How much cheese is left in pounds?

553. Christopher has a rope that is $\frac{2}{4}$ of a meter long. He needs to cut off $\frac{4}{9}$ of a meter to tie a knot. How long is the rope after the knot is tied?

554. Dylan has a rope that is $\frac{7}{8}$ of a yard long. He cuts off $\frac{1}{2}$ of the rope. How long is the remaining rope in yards?

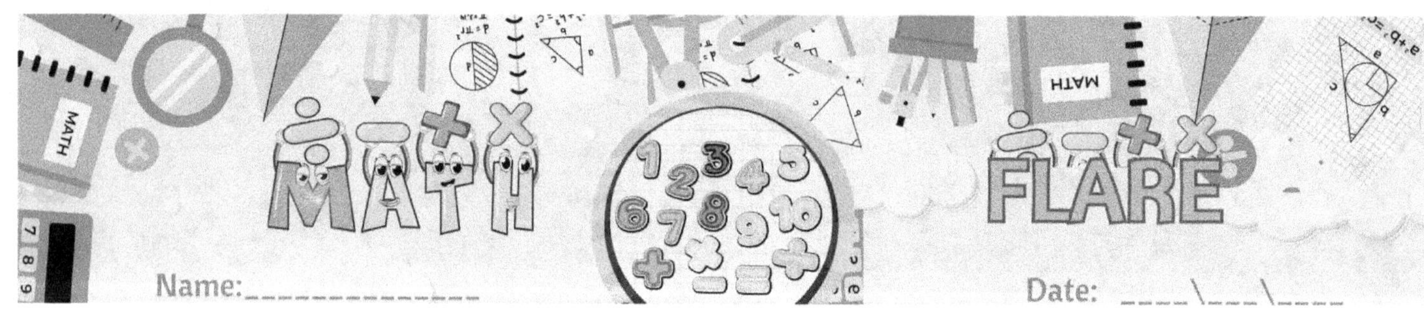

555. Brooklyn has $\frac{3}{10}$ of a pound of flour. She uses $\frac{1}{10}$ of the flour to make a pencake. How much flour is left in pounds?

556. Bella is making a sweet dish and needs $\frac{3}{4}$ of a cup of strawberries. She has already used $\frac{1}{6}$ of a cup. How much more strawberry does she need?

557. Sebastian has $\frac{5}{7}$ of a pizza left over from last night. He eats $\frac{1}{2}$ of the pizza for lunch. How much pizza does he have left?

558. Addison bought a bag of flour that weighed $\frac{5}{10}$ pounds. She used $\frac{1}{8}$ of the flour to make pencakes. How much flour was left in the bag?

559. Valentina is painting a room with a can of paint that has $\frac{1}{2}$ gallons in it. She has used $\frac{1}{5}$ of the paint so far. How much paint is left in the can?

560. A recipe calls for $\frac{6}{8}$ of a cup of milk. If $\frac{2}{4}$ of the milk is already used, how much milk is left in cups?

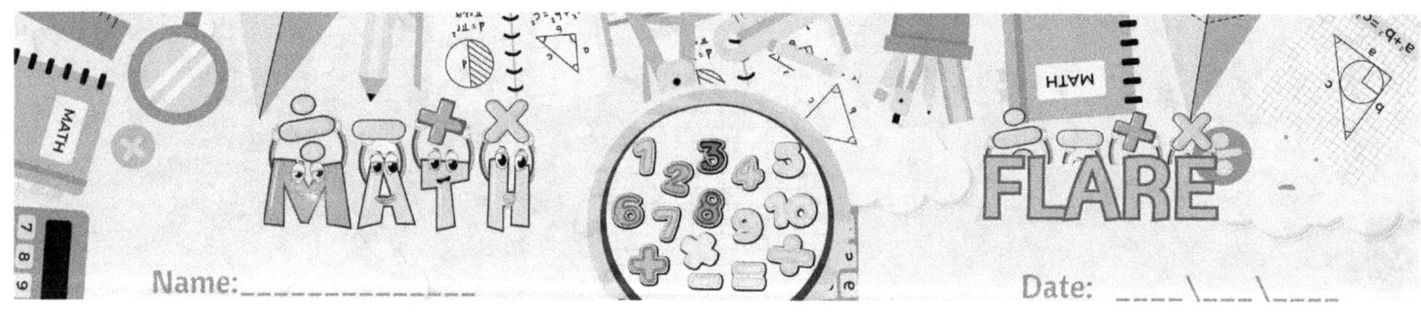

561. Reagan had $\frac{8}{10}$ of a cup of milk. If $\frac{1}{2}$ of the milk is spilled, how much milk is left in cups?

562. Isaac and Ariana are cooking dinner and need $\frac{5}{6}$ of a cup of oil. Isaac accidentally spills $\frac{3}{8}$ of a cup of oil. How much oil do they have left?

563. Vincent has a board that is $\frac{3}{5}$ feet long. He wants to cut off $\frac{1}{4}$ of the board. How long will the board be after the cut?

ANSWERS

Page 1:   Adding Decimals

1. 1,440.51	2. 1,032.76	3. 1,520.66	4. 893.55	5. 642.76
6. 903.02	7. 1,735.63	8. 1,392.86	9. 695.46	10. 792.29
11. 1,486.22	12. 1,102.62	13. 947.52	14. 1,103.64	15. 1,207.65
16. 1,598.72	17. 1,022.39	18. 871.00	19. 1,275.92	20. 693.48
21. 540.51	22. 978.99	23. 896.01	24. 1,819.24	25. 1,025.04
26. 1,514.95	27. 609.81	28. 1,563.74	29. 749.91	30. 1,181.32
31. 425.63	32. 1,676.42	33. 899.82	34. 1,367.73	35. 1,010.14
36. 1,109.70	37. 987.31	38. 650.18	39. 1,556.94	40. 423.52
41. 1,278.58	42. 1,102.73	43. 1,628.31	44. 1,365.70	45. 1,272.04
46. 1,176.99	47. 1,819.50	48. 1,287.61	49. 912.26	50. 434.50
51. 1,078.99	52. 1,412.56	53. 1,284.58	54. 545.18	55. 1,493.76
56. 647.61	57. 789.69	58. 444.22	59. 963.02	60. 971.12

Page 4:   Subtracting Decimals

61. 109.12	62. 58.54	63. 388.65	64. 696.97	65. 445.38
66. 254.89	67. 524.22	68. 423.73	69. 605.58	70. 343.77
71. 623.52	72. 390.14	73. 330.60	74. 82.99	75. 326.25
76. 198.26	77. 430.44	78. 2.63	79. 513.85	80. 799.55
81. 0.38	82. 16.94	83. 450.02	84. 576.79	85. 381.57
86. 103.53	87. 410.22	88. 402.49	89. 149.40	90. 352.22

91. 77.52	92. 507.87	93. 796.85	94. 635.23	95. 30.55
96. 271.23	97. 75.60	98. 619.37	99. 7.20	100. 2.00
101. 79.10	102. 51.60	103. 71.20	104. 419.74	105. 241.70
106. 98.16	107. 51.97	108. 515.15	109. 160.19	110. 339.56
111. 450.05	112. 528.70	113. 14.87	114. 536.65	115. 301.34
116. 59.12	117. 10.58	118. 24.31	119. 25.81	120. 470.64

Page 7: Multiplying Decimals

121. 680.40	122. 6,295.82	123. 3,625.76	124. 4,172.76
125. 929.19	126. 4,502.88	127. 5,516.49	128. 8,251.60
129. 2,500.02	130. 2,422.96	131. 1,354.65	132. 4,803.62
133. 3,683.73	134. 2,982.20	135. 1,639.47	136. 4,215.21
137. 3,721.20	138. 819.28	139. 3,411.01	140. 2,487.38
141. 1,200.54	142. 2,258.16	143. 6,422.28	144. 5,394.84
145. 7,894.35	146. 6,986.47	147. 2,180.40	148. 4,327.44
149. 1,090.25	150. 2,954.12	151. 2,216.52	152. 2,696.98
153. 346.32	154. 2,591.55	155. 4,157.01	156. 7,807.27
157. 2,333.02	158. 6,517.00	159. 1,058.50	160. 4,688.01
161. 3,149.16	162. 1,464.54	163. 4,824.49	164. 2,148.96
165. 4,142.58	166. 1,735.36	167. 496.86	168. 804.00
169. 2,509.20	170. 9,496.38	171. 653.52	172. 898.70
173. 1,405.50	174. 1,002.66		

Page 13: Dividing Decimals

175. 15.02	176. 41.7	177. 7.63	178. 25.8	179. 10.6
180. 1.96	181. 6.84	182. 21.55	183. 9.2	184. 12.0
185. 21.78	186. 8.27	187. 9.71	188. 9.24	189. 8.72
190. 3.22	191. 7.0	192. 3.65	193. 10.08	194. 5.9
195. 1.95	196. 9.04	197. 8.85	198. 15.23	199. 6.21
200. 3.66	201. 8.36	202. 18.76	203. 7.26	204. 4.72
205. 11.13	206. 14.36	207. 22.3	208. 47.25	209. 8.3
210. 4.3	211. 5.4	212. 9.7	213. 65.5	214. 11.67
215. 4.4	216. 9.45	217. 6.52	218. 14.45	219. 4.24

Page 18: Compare the Fractions

220. >	221. >	222. <	223. >	224. >	225. <	226. >	227. <
228. <	229. <	230. >	231. <	232. <	233. <	234. =	235. >
236. >	237. >	238. >	239. <	240. <	241. <	242. >	243. >
244. <	245. >	246. >	247. <	248. >	249. >	250. <	251. <
252. <	253. <	254. =	255. <	256. <	257. >	258. >	259. >
260. <	261. >	262. <	263. <	264. <	265. >	266. >	267. <
268. <	269. >	270. <	271. <	272. <	273. >	274. <	275. <
276. <	277. <						

Page 23: Equivalent Fractions

278. 24	279. 80	280. 4	281. 2	282. 8	283. 9	284. 24

285. 13   286. 1   287. 6   288. 52   289. 4   290. 56   291. 6

292. 12   293. 117   294. 10   295. 14   296. 11   297. 12   298. 18

299. 112   300. 5   301. 6   302. 10   303. 4   304. 10   305. 12

306. 2   307. 66   308. 14   309. 18   310. 20   311. 9   312. 2

313. 17   314. 13   315. 24   316. 128   317. 2   318. 130   319. 45

320. 5   321. 3   322. 6   323. 12   324. 5   325. 95   326. 6

327. 24   328. 13   329. 55   330. 18   331. 90   332. 114   333. 20

334. 7   335. 84

Page 28:   Fractions Addition: Common Denominator

336. 1/2   337. 4/5   338. 2/3   339. 6/7   340. 9/11   341. 5/6

342. 1/1   343. 7/9   344. 1/3   345. 3/4   346. 7/10   347. 4/5

348. 3/4   349. 2/3   350. 5/11   351. 1/2   352. 2/7   353. 5/7

354. 8/9   355. 4/5   356. 3/4   357. 3/5   358. 1/4   359. 9/11

360. 3/4   361. 3/8   362. 7/11   363. 9/10   364. 2/9   365. 5/12

366. 4/7   367. 1/3   368. 2/5   369. 2/3   370. 4/5   371. 9/11

372. 1/4   373. 1/3   374. 3/5   375. 6/7   376. 8/9   377. 5/6

378. 10/11   379. 5/9   380. 11/12   381. 3/5   382. 1/2   383. 6/7

384. 1/4   385. 7/11   386. 4/5   387. 1/2   388. 7/8   389. 3/10

390. 9/11   391. 9/10   392. 5/6   393. 5/9   394. 5/7   395. 5/8

Page 33:   Fractions Subtraction - Common Denominator

396. 3/11   397. 1/2   398. 2/9   399. 1/7   400. 1/3   401. 1/5

402. 1/12   403. 1/4   404. 1/2   405. 2/3   406. 3/11   407. 1/6

408. 1/7   409. 1/12   410. 2/5   411. 1/4   412. 1/8   413. 2/9

414. 3/11   415. 1/2   416. 1/12   417. 1/5   418. 1/7   419. 2/5

420. 2/7   421. 8/11   422. 1/3   423. 1/10   424. 1/4   425. 2/9

426. 5/7   427. 1/10   428. 1/3   429. 1/11   430. 2/3   431. 2/3

432. 5/8   433. 7/11   434. 1/8   435. 1/2   436. 2/5   437. 1/9

438. 1/2   439. 3/7   440. 1/12   441. 1/7   442. 1/3   443. 1/6

444. 1/5   445. 1/8   446. 1/12   447. 4/11   448. 2/9   449. 1/6

450. 3/8   451. 1/5   452. 1/6   453. 1/4

Page 38: Fractions Multiplication

454. 6/11   455. 5/8   456. 1/32   457. 50/91   458. 7/24

459. 1/3   460. 3/10   461. 2/7   462. 9/55   463. 64/117

464. 3/28   465. 2/5   466. 77/160   467. 1/6   468. 3/25

469. 5/16   470. 2/5   471. 1/8   472. 7/15   473. 36/77

474. 1/4   475. 35/96   476. 9/80   477. 1/10   478. 30/49

479. 1/15   480. 15/44   481. 1/15   482. 1/16   483. 5/8

484. 9/20   485. 49/156   486. 1/4   487. 112/135

Page 41: Fractions Division

488. 1   489. 8 1/4   490. 1/4   491. 5/9   492. 12/25

493. 1 1/6   494. 2 5/8   495. 11/25   496. 3/4   497. 5/16

498. 1 3/7   499. 3/5   500. 3/4   501. 1 5/7   502. 80/99

503. 7/8   504. 1 1/8   505. 9/40   506. 2 2/3   507. 1 10/11

508. 1/4   509. 1   510. 1/3   511. 1/2   512. 5 1/7

513. 4   514. 1 3/5   515. 25/32   516. 1/2   517. 1 1/3

518. 2/7   519. 1 3/4   520. 1 7/20   521. 7/11

Page 44: Fractions Addition Word Problems

522. 17/20   523. 7/10   524. 2/3   525. 43/56   526. 5/6

527. 29/35   528. 43/45   529. 11/15   530. 5/12   531. 9/10

532. 2/3   533. 31/35   534. 7/10   535. 50/63   536. 5/6

537. 5/12   538. 11/12   539. 11/14   540. 11/12   541. 7/10

542. 13/14

Page 51: Fractions Subtraction Word Problems

543. 1/10   544. 5/8   545. 1/10   546. 1/6   547. 1/2

548. 1/8   549. 1/40   550. 25/56   551. 1/3   552. 7/45

553. 1/18   554. 3/8   555. 1/5   556. 7/12   557. 3/14

558. 3/8   559. 3/10   560. 1/4   561. 3/10   562. 11/24

563. 7/20

www.ingramcontent.com/pod-product-compliance
Lightning Source LLC
Chambersburg PA
CBHW080722120726
48001CB00010B/3110